GW01117743

BLUE MOUNTAINS WILDERNESS

Blue Mountains Wilderness

Selections and Photographs by
David Liddle

Introduction by
Margaret Baker

a Megalong book

To the pioneers, the pathmakers and the poets...
to all those men and women who have contributed to our
understanding of the spirit of the Mountains.

a Megalong book
published by
Second Back Row Press Pty Ltd 1987
PO Box 43 Leura NSW 2781
Photographs copyright ©David Liddle
Text copyright ©Margaret Baker
Designed by Kevin Chan
Typeset by Tensor Type
Printed by Owen King Printers Australia Pty Ltd, Melbourne

ISBN 0909325510

PHOTOGRAPHER'S PREFACE

I think it is the silence of the Blue Mountains which impresses me most. It hits you like a wall when you stop. You can sit in the bush at the top of a great precipice and gaze right into that solid silence. You can see its edges in the whisper of gum leaves swaying in the vastness, and hear its great wisdom chanted from an ultra-distant waterfall. Grand realms of silence that quiver like a breast when an insect clatters over a nearby leaf and smoky silence that hovers like a fat hawk in the morning on the mist of a February valley. It is a penetrating silence which can make your bustling trouser legs sound like coal trucks while your feet are soundless on damp clay. Your own boots can shake that silence to its bones, echoing to the roots of the earth as you stomp up a spur. A twig snap one hundred metres away startles a bird and me, burgling this peace where we have been bathing our souls in a cocoon of utter quiet like butter melting in the sun and steeping our souls in the essence of the Mountains, as we rested and sifted the meaning of the great silence.

After that I suppose it is the subtlety. I mean, the Australian bush is so understated. Look at the colours. They are an elegy of muted greys and weathered greens. Battleship grey gum trees with bronze green leaves stand in khaki drill scrub; the 'heritage' colours of the hills. There is an infinite range of softened browns, dull russet rock on pale ochre soil.

The colours of the Mountains are more exciting because you have to look for them. Look at the colours to see their subtlety and spectacular understatement. After that you can see the lime green ferns in the valley, a red leaf on moss, white pebbles in a stream, new red and green eucalypt shoots and a bank of yellow wattle, the nude pink of Angophora flesh and the deep indigo of a buried dell.

Yet this subtlety is more than just colour. Australian marsupials are a timid lot and great stealth is required to observe a swamp wallaby in the twilight, great observation to spot a lizard by a rock, great awareness to notice the small detachments of honeyeaters migrating across the Mountains. You will have to be very early down a quiet path to see a lyrebird scoot by and need a great patience to understand the complexity of tiny lives that rage, ring and rest in a hanging swamp. You will hear wattle birds and magpies, whipbirds and bellbirds and see black cockatoos gliding and chirping about cliff tops, but you will have to watch closely for the little honeyeaters after banksia sap in winter and watch, as I did, in frozen awe as a great black snake oozed silently out of sight early one morning, vanishing into the very dew itself.

Even this grand landscape is so subtle. Some of the mightiest features do not become apparent until you stand right in front of them. On some of the little fenced walks around or under cliffs it is possible to be within a metre of a sheer vertical drop and not even see it. Look at Charles Darwin's approach to Wentworth Falls, how at first he was intrigued by a little then a little more until the magnificence of those great Falls burst upon him as he stood on their very brink. Yet to walk today through those rocks, across the stepping stones of the Jamison, down the paths and stairs under the cliffs is a symphony unimagined from above. It is orchestrated into minuets of pool, peak and fall as new vistas open one after another along a walk such as National Pass. It is possible to walk a living sonata of experience through Neates and Centennial Glens out to Beauchamp Falls, with deep movements and light passages in every theme. If you venture off the track anywhere out Narrow Neck, Shipley Plateau or McMahon's Point, it is easy to find something exciting and totally unsuspected only metres from where you were. Great worked rocks, trees, headlands, spurs and sights you would never suspect in our modest landscape.

This is the excitement of the Mountains for me. All that beauty, so quiet, so patient. It is as though it has waited here through aeons of time and creation, silent for centuries of centuries for this very special moment of insight when you first see it.

The Blue Mountains have many special moments and places. They are available to all for the effort of looking. Purple hills in the distance, jagged spurs overhanging sheer drops, crimson rosellas, art nouveau paths through cathedrals of fern, trees hanging with icicles, a spring gurgling under mossy bank, dew on casuarina needles, the cacophony of kookaburras at dawn in the Blue Gum Forest and bracing air which stirs great appetite. But tread carefully. These Blue Mountains can dazzle with vistas, intoxicate with the scent of flowers but confuse in spectacular canyons or elaborate underground caves, as at Jenolan. They can explode in summer bushfires and can lose a walker in miles of forest tramping. They can stir your blood in winter and have you weep at the beauty of a gum tree in spring.

Now it is important to say that despite their rugged grandeur, the Blue Mountains are not strictly a wilderness area in the purist sense. What I have photographed is the wildness of the Mountains and sometimes nature at work on the structures of man.

These Blue Mountains are so accessible, so near to civilisation and with so many approach paths, anyone can become familiar with many special environments for so little effort. They are a wilderness any family or pair of friends can discover whenever they have an hour or a day to play. Hardly a photograph in this book was taken more than a half day's walk from a railway, and none far from a formed track.

Thank you Jim Smith for pointing me down so many beautiful paths.

David Liddle
Balmain, January 1987

An Introduction To The Blue Mountains

An exquisite place
Ageless cathedrals of stone
Bathed in shimmering sunshine
Clothed in the softest hues......

Deep in the childhood memory of many a traveller is a special place, a place so impressive, so important, that its spirit takes possession of their soul and constantly draws them back. For me, that magical land is the Blue Mountains.

There are vivid recollections of Christmas holiday train journeys from Sydney's Central Station, through the dreary blur of suburban backyards and the relentless miles of low scrub baking in the heat of scorching summer days. Then suddenly, a new exhilaration. With a struggling climb from Emu Plains, the train bursts through the Glenbrook Tunnel into glorious mountain sunshine.

The wondrous warm yellows of Glenbrook Gorge and the mysterious blue haze of the shimmering forests that stretched as far as the eye could see beckoned us on through quaint villages, tiny specks in this vast wilderness. Weeks were spent exploring the delights of mountain walks, seeking moments of coolness in lush green, fern-clothed glades, experiencing the thrill of mountain waterfalls plunging their icy waters into crystalline pools below and searching for "devil heads" and milky chunks of quartz on the windswept ridges. We stood at Govett's Leap, immersed in the splendid panorama and shouted "coo-ee" from Echo Point to Mount Solitary. There were day trips to the Cathedral of Ferns at Mount Wilson, the jewel-encrusted wonders of Jenolan Caves where wallabies graced the Grand Arch, and to the tea rooms of the Megalong Valley for fresh scones and strawberry jam.

There were days, too, when the mountains dragged the clouds from the sky and a misty veil descended. We listened in the eerie stillness to the gentle drops from heavily laden leaves, and imagined where the Three Sisters should be. Memorable, too, were the first glimpses of snow on a cold August day. Rugged in warm scarves and coats, we made snowmen, our cheeks rosy red in the crisp mountain air.

These are the experiences of many who, like parents and grandparents before them, have escaped the surrounding plains to their special, private mountain hideaways. Many more are discovering the Mountains anew. These are the ever-increasing numbers of tourists, coach passengers, overseas visitors and bushwalkers who seek their own Mountains wilderness — the crisp clean air, breathtaking scenery that has been frozen in time by many an artist's brush, mossy stepping stones through ancient forests and cool ferny glades, grey swirling clouds of northward-bound swifts, plunging waterfalls and foaming cascades, or the solitude of secluded places where the intense silence of the Mountains is all-encompassing.

The Blue Mountains, a low sandstone plateau, rise from the flat Cumberland Plain west of Sydney to an altitude of 1100 metres. Their appearance from afar masks a remarkably dissected character.

"The visitor to the Blue Mountains, making the tour for the first time, scans the skyline for those contours that we generally associate with mountains. There are no towering summits and, save for an occasional hump, the horizon presents no imposing features. The gradual climb from the coastal flats at Emu Plains, up that remarkable dividing ridge to the Blue Mountains Plateau conveys little impression that an ascent is being made to nearly four thousand feet. It is only when you reach the precipitous brinks that almost entirely isolate this remarkable plateau that the full grandeur of the Blue Mountain region is dramatically revealed. Here are breathtaking panoramas of valleys walled in by perpendicular rock so deep that the giant forests below look like fluffy pile on a verdant carpet" (Frank Hurley, 1952).

It was not until after twenty-five years of European settlement of the colony of New South Wales that the first white people were able to experience the grandeur of this wilderness, suddenly and dramatically revealed from high vantage points. This deceptively even easterly extension of the Great Dividing Range, which Governor Phillip innocently named the Carmarthen and Lansdowne Hills, perplexed early explorers and presented an impenetrable barrier to westward extension of the colony.

The original inhabitants of this continent, the Aborigines, solved the mysteries of the labyrinthine valleys many thousands of years before. Archaeological evidence, "documents of stone", provides an incomplete but emerging picture of nomadic hunters and gatherers who roamed these mountains for perhaps 20,000 years. These people are thought to have been the Daruk, though there were Wiradjuri lands to the west and the Gandangara claimed the southern Blue Mountains.

Rock shelters in the upper Blue Mountains were occupied during the waning years of the world's last ice age. Though temperatures were low and winter snow regularly blanketed the plateau, the climate was drier than it is now, favouring habitation. Clothed in animal skins, the Aborigines settled in a snug, east-facing rock shelter on King's Table, Wentworth Falls, about 14,500 years ago and possibly even 7,500 years before that. As temperatures moderated, caves higher in the Mountains were sought and the spacious, river-cut Wall's Cave, near Blackheath, provided a temporary home 12,200 years ago.

The enfolding wilderness supplied a nourishing array of wild foods, including the swamp wallaby, grey kangaroo, possums, bandicoots, lizards, yabbies, platypus and shellfish. The fruits of the Geebung (*Persoonia sp.*) Lilly Pilly (*Acmena smithii*) and Native Raspberry (*Rubus parvifolius*), the fleshy roots of the Daisy Yam (*Microseris lanceolata*), and wild honey added seasonal variety to the diet.

Initially, Aboriginal population densities were low, with small family groups roaming over large areas. More permanent and denser settlement of favoured enclaves came with the introduction of a new, small stone tool technology and advanced techniques of food preparation. In the Capertee Valley and along the Nepean River, at least, the Burrawang (*Macrozamia communis*) became an important source of carbohydrate, once the toxins were removed from their bright-orange edible seeds. Fire, a tool used by Aborigines to modify their environment, was found to increase the size of Burrawang stands and their yield, and to promote simultaneous ripening. These discoveries may have permitted the plant to be used to support large gatherings of people on ceremonial occasions. Groups of Aborigines may have moved through the Blue Mountains to join in such festivals.

The traditional way of life of the Aborigines was rapidly and totally broken down by disease and displacement with the coming of Europeans. Their passing symbolised the fate of much of the world they knew. Memories of the Aborigines now remain only in scattered stone tools and artwork. Carved trees, mysterious arrangements of stones, coloured hand stencils, axe-grinding grooves, simple figured outlines of humans, animals and birds, and the emu tracks of the Cave Hotel on Bell's Line of Road (representative of the most ancient form of rock art), provide our only clues to the Blue Mountains' earliest inhabitants. Now archaeologists dig and tourists tread where ancient spirits dwell.

Although the Aborigines appear to have moved freely over the Blue Mountains and subsisted on its resources, history books chronicle only the attempts by European explorers, lacking the wisdom or experience of native generations, to conquer the Mountains.

In June 1789, Governor Phillip, standing at the junction of the Grose and Hawkesbury Rivers, prophesied that "shortly" their summits would be explored. Yet for many years more the colony's expansion was confined within its sandstone battlements, the cliffs defying all undertakings to tame them. Adventurous, determined of various backgrounds and motives, some seasoned explorers, were thwarted in their herculean efforts to solve the maze. These included an unknown number of escaped convicts, misguided by rumours that China lay on the other side of the mountains.

The first "official" attempted "crossings" were made by military personnel, who frequently employed quite inappropriate techniques. In December 1789, Naval Lieutenant William Dawes, accompanied by Lieutenant George Johnston and Surgeon's Mate Lowes, crossed the Nepean River and advanced along a compass bearing that led towards Round Hill (Mount Hay). The succession of ridges and deep ravines made such a march impractical and, faced with the impossibility of the terrain, they returned exhausted from Mount Twiss, north of Linden. "Dawes Ridge" commemorates this valiant excursion.

Captain William Paterson, a noted explorer of South Africa and a botanical correspondent with Sir Joseph Banks, was next to plan an expedition. In September 1793, with a small party, Paterson plunged his boats into the wilds of the Grose River, traversing boulders and waterfalls to struggle about fifteen kilometres upstream. Finally confronted by smashed boats and precipitous gorges near the confluence of the Grose and Wentworth Creek, he retreated. Paterson was not un-rewarded for his efforts — the Native Iris (*Patersonia*) celebrates his botanising achievements.

The adventurous seamen, Hacking and Bass, were next to set their sights on conquering the great barrier. The details of Hacking's August 1794 journey are not well known, but his reports of being driven back by wild and inaccessible terrain echo those of earlier adventurers. The account of George Bass's June 1796 expedition stirs the imagination. Loaded with scaling irons and ropes to conquer towering cliffs, he had obviously no thought in mind for road-builders who might follow. Bass is thought to have taken a southern route, through the Burragorang Valley and across the Wollondilly River into the wilds east of Kanangra Walls. "The horrible perpendicular....barren mountains affording them no means of supply they were reduced to a state of the most devouring thirst" (Else-Mitchell, 1951) and returned after fifteen days.

Francis Barrallier, an Ensign of the New South Wales Corps attempted, like Bass, a southern Blue Mountains crossing. He came within thirty kilometres of Jenolan Caves and in sight of the Boyd Plateau, after setting out on 22nd November, 1802. Barrallier, too, was unacquainted with the sustaining resources of the wilderness and after six days, with rapidly diminishing provisions and being unable to kill a fly, the party returned. Scaling waterfalls and "frightful precipices" with torn boots and injured feet, they were driven beyond the limits of endurance.

Interest was transferred again to the rugged northern mountains, with the proposed expedition by George Caley. Caley, a botanical collector for Sir Joseph Banks, was spurred on by an urge to penetrate further west than anyone else and the desire to collect specimens. Departing from the Hawkesbury on 3rd November 1804, he determined to reach the highest of the "Carmarthen Hills", which he named Mount Banks. A cursory glance of contour lines on modern topographic maps is convincing evidence of the incredibly difficult task faced by his party.

Caley's graphic journal account and descriptive place names add further to an appreciation of the frustrations presented by the soul-destroying terrain. We sense Caley's fear in the bushfire inadvertently started by his men on the edge of Burralow Swamp. We share, with sinking hearts, the prospect of the "Devil's Wilderness," that great and terrible cleft of the Grose which they had tried so hard to avoid. With parched throats we read of the desperate climb into this gorge, across Wilderness Brook, and out again. Clinging to narrow sandstone ledges, the men passed heavy luggage bundles from one to the other and quenched their thirsts, on that hot November day, with the acid fruit of the Native Currant (*Leptomeria acida*). Caley's disappointment at being forced to retrace his steps from Carmarthen Brook, when so close to Mount Banks, is vividly reflected in his depressing struggle through the damp undergrowth in the valley he named "Dismal Dingle." Finally, we rejoice with Caley at reaching the summit of Mount Banks, the object of his arduous journey.

The spirit of adventure that drove men on into wild terrain was soon to be replaced by the economic motive, the quest by leading figures of the colony to find new grazing lands. On 11th May 1813, Gregory Blaxland, a "gentleman farmer", William Lawson, who was pursuing a pastoral career, and William Charles Wentworth, then a grazier on the Nepean, set out on their journey from Blaxland's property at South Creek, near St. Marys. From reconnaissance journeys, Blaxland had determined that the successful route would follow the west ridge between the Grose and Warragamba Rivers. They may indeed have followed aboriginal tracks. On 28th May 1813, they stood on the edge of the western escarpment, later named Mount York by Governor Macquarie. Blaxland's "ridge theory" had proven correct. After descending into the grassy valley of the Cox's River, this famous three terminated their journey at Mount Blaxland, satisfied that the land stretching to the west could support the colony's stock for at least thirty years. This opinion was confirmed by George Evans, who surveyed the expedition route and continued on to the Macquarie River, where Bathurst now stands.

Construction of the first road across the Blue Mountains commenced on 18th July 1814, from Emu Plains, under the guidance of William Cox, the magistrate at Windsor. Completed on 14th January 1815, this twelve-foot wide "track" was a major engineering achievement. The terrain was difficult, the equipment primitive, and the labour unskilled. The descent from the western edge of the mountains into Hartley Vale proved most fustrating and the steepness of the road here became a cause of concern for travellers. Governor Macquarie noted that "the labour here undergone and the difficulties surmounted can only be appreciated by those who view this scene". Trees were tied behind carts to act as a brake on downhill runs, and ropes passed through rings in the rocks assisted in pulling vehicles up the slope. Ascents in wet weather were nightmarish.

New attempts were soon made to find easier routes. Lawson's Long Alley was constructed during 1822-1823 through a valley to the east of Cox's Road, but was steep and subject to flooding by Kerosene Creek. Lockyer's Road of 1828-1829, reaching for the intervening ridge, was never completed, the convict work-force being transferred to Victoria Pass. This latter road, completed under the guidance of Sir Thomas Mitchell in 1832, has remained in use ever since. It did prove too steep for early motor vehicles and was temporarily replaced (1912-1920) by Berghofer's Pass.

The four alternative routes are today N.S.W. Lands Department walking tracks. Walkers can admire the stone masonry and ingenuity of construction in tranquil forests that once echoed with the ring of pickaxes and vibrated with explosive charges.

The northern crossing of the Blue Mountains had to wait until September 1823, when nineteen year old Archibald Bell Jnr., with the help of a native, traversed the saddle connecting Mount Tomah and Mount Bell, circled the headwaters of the Grose and descended into the Vale of Clwydd, joining Cox's Road near Collit's Inn. The conquest of the wilderness had begun.

Thus the sandstone cliffs, within whose enclaves the Aborigines sought shelter, rebuffed the early European explorers and hampered road and railway builders. These majestic golden walls, which stand as fortresses guarding the hazy blue valleys, concealed the mystery of their origins and confounded early scientific investigators.

Charles Darwin, on his famous world voyage in "The Beagle", traversed the Blue Mountains in January 1836. His initial reaction was one of disappointment:

"From so grand a title as Blue Mountains and from their absolute altitude, I expected to have seen a bold chain of mountains crossing the country; but instead of this, a sloping plain presents merely an inconsiderable front to the low land near the coast."

His complaint soon turned to rapture, however, and his elation on encountering the Jamison Valley at "The Weatherboard" (now Wentworth Falls) would surely inspire any travellers:

"Following down a little valley and its tiny rill of water, an immense gulf unexpectedly opens through the trees which border the pathway, at a depth of perhaps 1500 feet. Walking on a few yards, one stands on the brink of a vast precipice, and below one sees a grand bay or gulf, for I know not what other name to give it, thickly covered with forest. The point of view is situated as if at the head of a bay, the line of cliff diverging on each side, and showing headland behind headland, as on a bold sea-coast. These cliffs are composed of horizontal strata of whitish sandstone, and are so absolutely vertical, that in many places a person standing on the edge and throwing down a stone, can see it strike the trees in the abyss below. So unbroken is the line of cliff, that in order to reach the foot of the waterfall, formed by this little stream, it is said to be necessary to go sixteen miles around. About five miles distant in front, another line of cliff extends, which thus appears completely to encircle the valley...This kind of view was to me quite novel, and extremely magnificent."

Darwin's enthusiasm increased as he continued his journey:

"very early in the morning I walked about three miles to see Govett's Leap: a view of similar character with that near the Weatherboard, but perhaps even more stupendous. So early in the day the gulf was filled with a thin blue haze, which although destroying the general effect of the view, added to the apparent depth at which the forest was stretched out beneath our feet. These valleys which so long presented an insuperable barrier to the attempts of the most enterprising of the colonists to reach the interior, are most remarkable...But the most remarkable feature in their structure is, that although several miles wide at their heads, they generally contract towards their mouths to such a degree as to become impassable."

An earlier visitor, Governor Lachlan Macquarie, on his official tour of the Blue Mountains in 1815, was likewise impressed with the area to the south of The Weatherboard. His Secretary, J.T. Campbell, wrote:

"The majestic grandeur of the situation, combined with the various objects to be seen from this place, induced the Governor to give it the appellation of the King's Table-land. On the south-west side of the King's Table-land the Mountain terminated in abrupt precipices of immense depth, at the bottom of which is seen a glen, as romantically beautiful as can be imagined, bounded on the further side by Mountains of great magnitude, terminating equally abruptly as the others; and the whole thickly covered with timber. The length of this picturesque and remarkable tract of country is about twenty four miles, to which the Governor gave the name of The Prince Regent's Glen."

Journeying to another hill, Macquarie obtained an expanded view of the south-west side of the Prince Regent's Glen — a view which was "particularly beautiful and grand. Mountains rising beyond mountains, with stupendous masses of rock in the foreground, here strike the eye with admiration and astonishment. The circular form in which the whole is so wonderfully disposed, induced the Governor to give it the name of Pitt's Amphitheatre. The wondrous ravines and the rocks of the lofty cliffs defied explanation."

On 22nd May 1813, Blaxland, Lawson and Wentworth had attempted, unsuccessfully, the descent into the Jamison Valley from King's Tableland, hoping to procure "specimens of the different Stones and Minerals of the country." They considered that this "broken rocky Country" had been formed by "an earthquake or some dreadful Convulsion of Nature." Charles Darwin offered a different explanation:

"The first impression, on seeing the correspondence of the horizontal strata on each side of these valleys and great amphitheatrical depressions, is that they have been hollowed out, like other valleys, by the action of water; but when one reflects on the enormous amount of stone, which on this view must have been removed through mere gorges or chasms, one is led to ask whether these spaces may not have subsided. But considering the form of the irregularly branching valleys, and of the narrow promontories projecting into them from the platforms, we are compelled to abandon this notion. To attribute these hollows to the present alluvial action would be preposterous;... I imagine that the strata were heaped by the action of strong currents, and of the undulations of an open sea, on an irregular bottom, and that the valley like spaces thus left unfilled had their steeply sloping flanks worn into cliffs, during a slow elevation of the land; the worn down sandstone being removed, either at the time when the narrow gorges were cut by the retreating sea, or subsequently by alluvial action."

A Dreamtime legend related by Mel Ward gives a contrasting view of the origins of the Blue Mountains area:

"According to the Aborigines the whole region was a flat plain with only a great lake in the middle. Living in that lake was a gigantic monster, half reptile and half fish, with eyes the size of the moon, and they shone like the moon. Its name was Garangatch.

Also living on the plain was a giant, half wild cat, half man, whose name was Mirrigan.

One day while Mirrigan was hunting over the plain, he saw the eyes of Garangatch shining in the lake, and he threw his great spear at him. But Garangatch dived and the spear missed him. Mirrigan then collected bark off the trees to poison the water of the lake and kill the giant, but Garangatch dived deeper and the poison did not reach him, so Mirrigan went off for more bark.

While Mirrigan was away from the edge of the lake Garangatch, deciding to leave the lake for the first time in his life, came to the bank and threw himself onto the land. Now, he was so vast in size and so heavy, that the land would not support him and his vast body cut its way through the surface of the plain like a great plow, thus cutting all the valleys and casting up the rocks and earth on each side, slapping them with his fins and tail, forming the flat cliff faces. The water of the lake followed him and made the Cox's River.

Garangatch ended up in a natural lake beyond Oberon which they say is bottomless, consequently Mirrigan could never disturb Garangatch again. He is still safe in that lake they tell me, but mind you I wouldn't disturb him if I was you...."

The origins of these Mountains are no longer lost in the misty veils of creation, but form one of the last pieces in the jigsaw of the Australian continent. Fashioned thousands of millions of years after the emergence of the first solid crust, the rock strata provide a fascinating history of changing environments — of cold shallow seas, marshy shorelines, volcanic eruptions, giant flooding streams and the wrenching apart of drifting continents. Walks from the deepest valleys to the ridges above graphically reveal the pages of this history.

The Blue Mountains make up the western edge of the Sydney Basin which formed about 300-280 million years ago when Australia was still part of Gondwana, the great southern continent, and drifting towards the polar regions. Marine silts, exposed in the depths of the Grose and Jamison Valleys, were soon covered by sediments of an emerging coastline. Long, flat, deltaic shorelines of deciduous *Glossopteris* swamp forests seasonally provided the thick accumulations of vegetative material which consolidated into coal deposits. These Permian Coal Measures, formed around 280-250 million years ago, and displayed along the gentler scree-covered slopes below the main cliffline, were the object of the early coal and oil shale mining industries of the Mountains. Some five to ten million years later, during the Triassic period, south-east Australia had drifted to the South Pole, though no ice was accumulated. Left as a legacy of stream deposits are the sandstone-dominated layers (Caley Formation) of the well-vegetated zone at the base of the cliffs, familiar to walkers of Federal Pass. Earth movements to the north initiated a dramatic change to this ancient environment. Quartz-rich sands from braided streams flooded into the area, covering the Sydney Basin for at least ten million years, and cemented to form the Narrabeen Sandstones, those wondrous vertical cliffs of the upper Blue Mountains.

The changing balance of the land saw a corresponding shift in stream direction, and great braided streams from the south-west deposited the sands which became Hawkesbury Sandstone, the cliff-maker of the lower Blue Mountains. Under the weight of sediment the basin subsided further to allow an invasion by the sea about 220 million years ago, blanketing the sands with Ashfield Shale, which is confined primarily to the lower Mountains. Intrusions of volcanic material about 150 million years ago, during the Jurassic period, may have signalled the start of a very unsettled phase. We are now left with circular valleys, often clothed with ferns, like Murphy's Glen. About 95 million years ago, New Zealand started to break free from Australia, as the Tasman Sea formed. The Eastern Highlands were consequently uplifted, though they extended over a wider area than at present. Associated volcanic activity later produced the fissure basalts which now form the cappings of the highest sections of the northern Blue Mountains, including Mounts Banks, Tomah, Wilson and Hay. The Eastern Highlands achieved their present extent about 65 million years ago, when coastal regions subsided. The ages of the Kurrajong Fault and the Lapstone Monocline, major features determining the structure of the eastern escarpment of the Blue Mountains, are still to be determined accurately.

The seeming stability of the Blue Mountains plateau masks a very active past, and an antiquity which exceeds that of the world's highest mountain range, the Himalayas. The Himalayas, like other great fold mountains, have majestic, lofty, snow-covered peaks; the Blue Mountains, by contrast, have breathtaking, cavernous, forest-green depths.

But what of the fine detailing of the Blue Mountains; the formation of deep valleys and rocky crags, and the etching of bizarre features in stone? We need not evoke the role of earthquakes or oceanic activity as earlier writers have done, but simply observe the very processes evident now. The slope of the valleys is determined by the constituent rocks of the region. Because the Sydney Basin was sinking under the weight of its sediments, the edges are raised like the rim of a saucer and older rocks are exposed at progressively higher elevations. Rock strata also tend to thin towards the west. Mountain streams have cut through the hard sandstones into the softer bands of Permian rocks. Weathering processes known as "sapping" then concentrated on the softer layers, which were eroded away, leaving behind unsupported massive sandstone blocks. These slipped downwards along vertical joints or cracks to form the slope below the cliff line. Dramatic evidence of this form of mass-movement was provided in 1931 by the Katoomba Landslide. Sapping occurs wherever claystone and shale interbed with sandstone, as in the red band of Mt. York claystone about halfway down the cliffs, separating two major layers of Narrabeen Sandstone. Here, weathering of claystone and the collapse of the unsupported sandstone produce a marked benching of the cliffs, which lends itself to walking tracks and is easily identified from afar by its associated line of vegetation. The double fall of many Blue Mountains waterfalls is due to the presence of claystone.

The double-angled valley sides of the upper Blue Mountains owe their existence to the presence of different rock strata. The vertical cliffs are formed from hard Narrabeen Sandstones, while the lower, more gentle slopes, are of softer Permian rocks. The wearing back of slopes has produced the awe-inspiring amphitheatres for which the Mountains are justly famous. Popular tourist attractions like the Three Sisters, Orphan Rock, Mount Solitary and the Ruined Castle are spectacular remnants of these processes, as are the mysterious sandstone "pagodas" of the upper Grose Valley.

The streams which ultimately remove the rock debris from the Mountains leap in dramatic cascades from the plateau surfaces to the wilds below. Vaulting in rainbow sprays, these formerly gentle, fern-lined streams thunder onto giant boulders and swirl in icy plunge pools, watering the ancient stands of rainforest that cluster around moss-covered banks.

To the west of the Blue Mountains, in the Megalong and Hartley Valleys, exposed ancient granites form a terrain of marked contrast to the lofty battlements. The landscape, though softer, has its own charm, and memorable is the sight of the Casuarina-lined Cox's River flowing around massive rounded granite boulders, while platypus dart from its banks.

Just as these dramatic landforms have drawn both visitors and residents to the Mountains, so their characteristic climate has attracted wide praise. Many extoll the virtues of its fresh, invigorating air, and this region was once considered an ideal site for hospitals and sanitoria, as well as holiday homes. Yet the cool, moist climate is punctuated by the climatic extremes which plague much of Australia. Waterfalls, which are reduced to a mere trickle during drought, can become raging torrents after heavy rainfall. By contrast, savage summer north-westerly winds bring the threat of bushfire, striking fear into the hearts of Mountains dwellers.

The upper Blue Mountains are renowned for their mist that may drift about for days. One moment it lifts to reveal tantalising glimpses of an almost forgotten landscape, with bare cliffs highlighted in gold by shafts of sunlight, then it descends again, playing tricks with our imagination. Huge cottonwool drifts of vapour fill the valleys like clouds that have lost their way.

For a few days each year snow blankets the Mountains, transforming them into a fairytale world. On a freezing day in July 1986, with icy winds blasting from Antarctica, my companions and I shared a unique experience. The extraordinarily cold night left many waterfalls frozen, and we stood in awe at the sight of Wentworth Falls, completely ice-bound, like a spreading bridal veil. Snow covered the ridges and ice encrusted the trees and bushes. Delicately engraved ice crystals formed around the Coral Ferns and long ice swords encased the drooping leaves of the *Gahnias*. Frozen stalactites clung tenuously to rock overhangs and helictital forms curved in mysterious shapes. Every turn in the track brought a new wonderment — magical lands where the oreads silently played. The peace was shattered briefly by the deafening crash of huge blocks of the frozen falls, dislodged by the awakening sun, and the tinkling plunge of jewelled daggers that threatened life and limb.

Other worlds may be uncovered amid the plant-life of the Mountains, which is intricately linked to the fauna it supports. The location of both is determined by the complex interaction of geology, landforms, soil, climate and fire frequency. A rare floral display, remarkable in its subtlety, clothes the ridges and valleys. Nurtured in this wilderness are plant species found only in the Blue Mountains, some exceedingly rare and endangered.

As the vegetation of the steep valleys initially proved inaccessible, the early travellers became acquainted only with the life forms of the ridge tops. When Blaxland, Lawson and Wentworth reached Kings Tableland they saw it as two thousand acres clear of trees, covered with loose stones and short coarse grass, much like some commons in England. Renee Lesson, on his journey of 1824, noted "on the bare sandstone strata of the Kings Tableland the vegetation is stunted, yet you may see there different kinds of Casuarina, Eucalyptus, Melaleuca etc." These are the heathlands which thrive on the rockiest ledges of windswept cliff edges and ridge tops. Growing in poor shallow soil, the low plants are toughened and stunted, with thickened, gnarled stems and reduced, leathery leaves. Eucalypts adopt here a many-branched mallee form.

From autumn to early summer the heathlands present an unrivalled show of wildflowers. Venture onto Kings Tableland in early winter and enjoy the striking bright-orange cylindrical spikes of Heath Banksia (*Banksia ericifolia*), each with its complement of nectar-seeking honeyeaters, or catch your breath on the sweet perfume of *Acacia suaveolens* and search among the rocky crags for the dwarfed form of the Cypress, *Callitris muelleri*. Descend in spring from the heights of Mount Banks through a floral treasure trove. Here the purples of *Patersonia sericea* and *Sowerbaea juncea*, the stunning burgundy female flowers of *Allocasuarina nana*, the fragile white petals of *Mitrasacme polymorpha* and the familiar "eggs-and-bacon" yellow and reds of *Mirbelia platylobioides* create a superb rockery among the toughest plates of sandstone.

Hanging swamps occur where drainage is hindered. Swamp plants grow on thick peaty deposits which perch on impervious rock layers. Of amazing fragility, these cling tenuously to clifftops above the deep vales that threaten to engulf them. The wet conditions, while attracting a special plant community of rushes, sedges and small shrubs, exclude the growth of eucalypts. The insect-eating *Utricularia dichotoma* and red *Drosera spathulata* colour the edges of the swamp amid a tangled confusion of *Gleichenia dicarpa*, the ancient Coral Fern, the Mountains' own pink *Grevillea acanthifolia*, the densely packed, soft pink flowers of *Sprengelia incarnata* and the vibrant blue, veined Sun Orchid (*Thelymitra venosa*). Raising their yellow heads on slender stalks are *Acacia ptychoclada* and *Xyris gracilis*. A special treat for summer walkers is a rare glimpse of Christmas Bells (*Blandfordia spp.*), nodding their glorious red and gold flowers on erect stems above the mass of swamp-dwelling plants. Many small birds visit the swamps for insects, seeds and nectar. Grevillea and Hakea flowers attract honeyeaters, while thornbills and wrens hunt insects through the tangle.

The early European settlers recognised the hanging swamps as a valuable source of food for horses, and of fresh water. The Aborigines sought the swamp wallaby, native rodents, marsupial mice and yabbies from their marshy homes. We, too, now acknowledge the importance of these giant sponges of soil and matted vegetation in slowly releasing water to creeks, waterfalls and plants below, providing a constant flow to our water storage systems.

Eucalypt woodland and open forests, from which emanate the oil droplets that scatter sunlight and turn the Mountains "blue", dominate the sandy ridges and dry valley slopes. Low twisted forms of the darkly furrowed Black Ash (*Eucalyptus sieberi*) and Sydney Peppermints (*Eucalyptus piperita*), which bear spectacular summer blossoms, shelter a wonderful profusion of flowering shrubs. White waves of *Pimelea* and billowing yellow breezes of *Pomaderris* drift across the clifftops in spring.

The silvery blue-green flower spikes of *Banksia serrata*, the brilliant yellow globular flowers of *Acacia terminalis*, the snowy white *Eriostemon hispidulus*, deep pink *Boronia ledifolia* and the familiar red of Mountain Devil (*Lambertia formosa*) colour any walk. Look closely on the ground for tiny native orchids, for they are plentiful here too. But the crowning jewel of these forests is the Waratah (*Telopea speciosissima*), whose beauty was extolled by Louisa Anne Meredith, a journeyer here in 1839:

"I had often been told of the 'waratah', and its grand appearance when growing; and as we drove along, instantly recognised from the description the first of these magnificent flowers we saw ... The stem is woody, and grows perfectly straight, from three to six feet in height, about the thickness of a walking cane, and bearing rich green leaves ... all the way up. At the top of this stem is the flower, entirely of the brightest and richest shade of crimson-scarlet. A circle of large spreading petals forms its base, from which rises the cone or pyramid of trumpet-like florets, three, four, or five inches high ... Sometimes the stems branch off like a candelabrum, but more generally the flowers grow singly, one on each stalk, and look like bright flambeaux amidst the dark recesses of these wild forests ... The few plates I have seen give but a very faint idea of this most stately and regal flower."

Bird life abounds, adding to the joy of these forests. Parties of grey and red Gang-gang Cockatoos spread gumnut debris from the crowns of eucalypts, and Crimson Rosellas crack open the hard seeds of Casuarina and Acacia with their sharp beaks. Tree creepers dart up tree trunks, seeking insects, and tiny pardalotes and striated thornbills forage in the treetops. Kookaburras dwell in the hollows of mottle-barked Scribbly Gums (*Eucalyptus sclerophylla*) which also provide possums with a home.

The opening of valley walking trails revealed to visitors a cool escape from the summer heat of the ridges. Even the apparently barren, dry, vertical cliff walls have their own charm. Walkers descending Katoomba's Giant Stairway in spring are greeted by a highly specialised group of plants — the cliff-face dwellers. Clumps of vivid white *Sprengelia monticola*, fine sprays of *Allania endlicheri*, spikes of *Dracophyllum secundum*, deep pink splashes of *Epacris reclinata* and the glistening twin forks of *Drosera binata* catch the eye and appeal to the senses.

In the multi-hued spray of waterfalls, cliff faces drip with moist ferns. Some shelter and nourish *Microstrobos fitzgeraldii*, a rare conifer found only in the spray zones of six Blue Mountains waterfalls. The ancient Coral Fern forms interlacing banks and the finely divided fronds of the King Fern *(Todea barbara)* grace rock crevices and the edges of cool, sandy pools.

Early guide books exploited such ferny glades in attracting tourists. The Railway Guide of 1894 describes Wentworth Falls thus:

"After running over its rocky bed, the stream, which varies in volume according to the rainfall, flows on until it sweeps gracefully over the projecting semi-circular ledge of the Weeping Rock, and plunges in white foam upon the hollow sandstone bed some twenty feet beneath, from whence it playfully emerges, then hurries on its way to the Queen's Cascade, and glides over the Golden Sands to the final fall. Behind the veil of water which supplies the Weeping Rock with its flood of crystal tears, is a cool grotto filled with a luxuriant growth of ferns, the green and bronzed fronds of which form a delicately picturesque background. To the right, at the foot of a flight of steps, there nestles an ever-moist bed of ferns, which not to the credit of tourists who fail to observe the sixth commandment, have to be protected from vandalism by a barbed wire fence. The whole of the rocky glen through which the waters run over the cascades, and whose banks are clothed with coarse grasses, verdant shrubs, and ti-tree brush, is a lovely little natural cutting, leading to the tremendous valley beyond."

In the "tremendous" valleys beyond are forests which thrive in moist, sheltered, deep soil. The largest trees in the Blue Mountains grow here, forming tall, open forests. Here we are dwarfed by the giant Brown Barrels *(Eucalyptus fastigata)* of Leura Forest and the massive circumference of the Turpentine *(Syncarpia glomulifera)* trunks along Federal Pass, which tower over glades of tree ferns and shade-loving shrubs. Rejoice in the mottled bark of *Eucalyptus deanei* in the Blue Gum Forest on the Grose River, and seek out wombats under the purple drifts of *Indigofera australis* on the upper slopes of Mount Banks. The white, solitary forms of the familiar Mountain Ash *(Eucalyptus oreades)* stand like silent sentinels on cliff-face ledges. Lyrebirds churn through leaf litter for insects, and a collection of blue straws means that a Satin Bowerbird is not far away.

In the darkest cliff enclaves, sprayed by plunging waterfalls, tall, open eucalypt forests are replaced by rainforests which still shelter species surviving from Gondwanaland. To enter their shaded stillness is to experience another world. Straight growing, thin-barked trunks, broad, soft leaves and an open, damp, leaf-littered floor contrast markedly with the ridge-top forests. When viewed from above, the closed canopy of dark green leaves sets the rainforest apart, particularly in summer when highlighted by the cream-turning-to-pink "flowers" of the Coachwood *(Ceratopetalum apetalum)*.

Many visitors to the Mountains first discover the rainforest at the base of Katoomba Falls. Coachwoods, Sassafras *(Doryphora sassafras)*, Sweet Pittosporum *(Pittosporum undulatum)* and the delicate Cedar Wattle *(Acacia elata)* intermingle as a dense cover above the forest floor. Black Wattle *(Callicoma serratifolia)* and the Rough Tree Fern *(Cyathea australis)* grow luxuriously in the dappled light. The Wonga Pigeon may be seen feeding on the drooping clusters of dark blue berries of the Blueberry Ash *(Elaeocarpus reticulatus)* and on the Wonga Vine *(Pandorea pandorana)* which scrambles into the canopy in search of light.

A magical stand of rainforest in the Grand Canyon is traversed by the track from Evans Lookout to Neates Glen, at Blackheath. The very deep, narrow valley of Greaves Creek shelters a botanical wonderland — ancient Coachwood giants with distinctive, pink-blotched trunks form a dense canopy with fine specimens of Sassafras. Lilly Pilly, Possumwood *(Quintinia sieberi)* and Pepper Bush *(Tasmannia insipida)* provide a layer beneath, and the shade and moisture of the rainforest floor support mosses, fungi and ferns. The King Fern grows luxuriantly along the banks of Greaves Creek, while *Microsorum scandens* seeks the sunlight along the tree trunks. This is a silent world of dappled light and shaded, mythical forms...tread softly!

The Blue Mountains environment is unquestionably a unique assemblage of natural features, and as the settlement of Sydney grew, changing perceptions of its value began to emerge.

Cox's Road linked the coastal settlement of Sydney with the western pastures of the Bathurst district, the Mountains serving merely as a communication artery. Early military depots and inns, which protected and served western-bound travellers, often formed the foundations for future town developments. Services expanded during the 1850s as fortune seekers passed through on their way to the goldfields.

The new railway, an engineering feat which is a tribute to John Whitton, was completed to The Weatherboard in July 1867 and to Mt. Victoria in May 1868. It provided a relatively reliable and rapid form of transport for those with the leisure time and resources to escape from the health problems of the coastal settlement. By the mid 1870s Sydney's death rate from disease was increasing. Unsewered, overcrowded, poorly ventilated buildings spread the fear of cholera, typhoid and smallpox. The Mountains offered the chance for escape. Lofty heights, healthier mountain sunlight, rarefied, invigorating air and the antiseptic vapour of eucalypts were thought to be of considerable benefit, and so were used to promote the Blue Mountains into the 1930s and again more recently.

Sanatoria, resorts and hydropathic baths were established.

Country homes were sought by the eminent of Sydney. Sir Henry Parkes settled at Faulconbridge, Sir John See at Yester Grange, Wentworth Falls, and the Fairfax Family at Mt. Victoria. The recreational advantages of the Blue Mountains received much impetus in 1879 with the publication of the first Railway Guide of New South Wales. Gracious hotels and guesthouses, established from the 1880s, provided accommodation for holidaymakers who sought the scenic pleasures promised. Of the hotels, the Carrington (formerly the Great Western Hotel from 1882-1886) and the Hydro Majestic, opened by Mark Foy in 1904, remain today.

The *Picturesque Atlas of Australia*, the railway guides and the albums of commercial photographs gave their greatest attention to Govett's Leap, Blackheath, and Wentworth Falls.

"Their patronage was made possible by the nearby public railway platforms and was spurred by the athletic conventions of the day, of which they were an embodiment. The cult of the Sublime and the Beautiful reigned: it revered a vast panorama of awesome cliffs and chasmic valleys. Social conviction held that Nature taught Mankind and that the greatness of mountains served to impress with the sense of man's own littleness." (Anne Burke, 1985).

To increase the accessibility and attraction of sights, tracks were cleared, steps etched into cliff faces and lookouts constructed. These activities were first undertaken at Govett's Leap by a local Progress Committee in the 1880s. Here, T. Williams and his son, using several tons of explosives, constructed steps to the bottom of the falls. Completed after seven months and at a cost of £140, this path, whose undertaking had been deemed impossible, was opened on 25th January 1889. It was extended as a circular walk to Evans Lookout by February 1900 and named Rodriguez Pass after its promoter, Blackheath Stationmaster T.R. Rodriguez. Described as passing through the most romantic piece of country in the Commonwealth, the Grand Canyon, the walk from Wall's Cave to Evans Lookout joined Rodriguez Pass in 1907. Meanwhile, at Wentworth Falls, the track from the Valley of the Waters to the falls was begun in 1890. Five men completed this task under the direction of Captain Murray who, it is said, let a man over the side of the cliff on a rope to mark out the plan of the steps. At a lower level, National Pass was traced from Wentworth Falls to the Valley of the Waters and opened in 1908.

Prior to the completion of National Pass, interest had shifted to the Katoomba-Leura area, linked by the Federal Pass in 1900. This walking trail was seen as a prime commercial asset to the two towns. Its construction was part of a deliberate policy of development by the Katoomba Municipal Council, with the aim of attracting greater business to the town. Bowling greens, municipal baths and the Leura Golf Club were soon to follow. The newly emerging consumer-oriented, middle-class visitors from Sydney, who became the "backbone of tourism" were not to be attracted by the mere contemplation of nature!

Katoomba's commercial beginnings dated from the 1870s, with the extraction of the coal and oil shale deposits of the Jamison and Megalong Valleys. It was previously known only for its stone quarry, "The Crushers". Continued intermittently and with varying results, mining activity brought the Katoomba region to wider public notice, and left the legacy of a railway haulage system, now the "Scenic Railway", which plunges tourists daily into Pitt's Amphitheatre.

The Mountains, and Katoomba particularly, were the site for an increasing number of private guest houses. Daily coaches ran through the summer months to favoured scenic spots, and leisurely bushwalking continued as a popular activity. But change was in the air, perhaps precipitated by the appearance of the Three Sisters on the front page of the 1912 *Official Tourist Guide*. These characteristic erosion remnants, which were newly achieving individual prominence, became the logo of the Mountains, patronised by famous Katoomba photographer Harry Phillips. As Katoomba became the honeymoon mecca in the early 1920s, the tranquil ferny glades were overshadowed by the romanticisation of the cliff-top vantage points.

The 1930s depression saw the construction of the projecting platform at Echo Point, the Prince Henry Cliff Walk, and the floodlighting of Bridal Veil Falls, Leura Cascades, Katoomba Falls, the Three Sisters and Orphan Rock. Motor vehicles sped people from sight to sight. To gaze from the ridges, that preoccupation of a century before, had again become the way to experience the landscape. The Giant Stairway, one relic of the 1930s more reminiscent of earlier days, survives with deserved popularity. With steps hewn out of the perpendicular cliff face, extending from the Three Sisters to the Dardanelles Track, it serves as a fine monument to Chief Ranger Jim McKay, an enthusiastic track builder.

The depression also brought a revival in hiking and serious bushwalking, and the modern conservation movement is said to date from that period. During the Easter holidays of 1931, Alan Rigby led a party of Mountain Trails Club and Sydney Bushwalkers to the Blue Gum Forest, where they chanced on the planned beginnings of forest ringbarking for the purpose of planting walnuts. Rightly enraged at the threatened destruction, they commenced negotiations with the lessee, Mr. C.A. Hungerford, who agreed to cease operations for a cash payment of £150. Considerable fund-raising followed, a difficult task in economically depressed times. But success was theirs, and on 2nd September 1932, the forty acre (sixteen hectare) area was proclaimed a public recreation reserve, with trustees appointed from walking clubs. Myles Dunphy and others involved in this campaign then worked towards establishing the Blue Mountains National Park, a scheme originally formulated in 1922. Finally gazetted in 1959, and later enlarged, the Blue Mountains National Park now contains within its boundaries much of the remaining wilderness.

Following the Second World War, many changes took place in the Blue Mountains. Improvements in the performance of motor vehicles, electrification of the railway by 1957, and availability of relatively cheap land, led to a rapid increase in the residential population. This trend shows no signs of abating, and many Mountains towns are but extensions of suburban Sydney. It is rarely possible to stand at a lookout and gaze at a view where "neither roof nor road scars the eternal green over which there hangs a perpetual veil of blue haze", as did Frank Hurley in 1952.

Considerable environmental stresses have accompanied the population increase. These include the loss of natural plant cover, weed infestations of bushland, siltation of once deep mountain pools, pollution of streams, drainage of hanging swamps so that many waterfalls are reduced to a trickle, and the encroachment of buildings on the escarpment. All is not well, but our Mountains paradise is not irretrievable.

Recreational use of the area is changing. The trend has been towards rushed day visits, and provision of facilities and entertainment for day trippers and coach tourists who congregate briefly at a few selected cliff-top scenic points and picnic areas. The recent refurbishing of guesthouses and restaurants represents an effort to promote a more leisurely, relaxed enjoyment of the Blue Mountains.

Changes are also taking place in the valleys. Attempts are being made to encourage greater recreational use of walking tracks, many of which have become neglected, overgrown and in disrepair. Private guiding organisations are emerging and walking guides being trained, while the National Parks and Wildlife Service offers a varied walks programme during school holidays. For those who have always sought beauty and solitude in the Mountains, however, official revival of old tracks is too slow. The acclamation by government officials, aldermen and royalty, which accompanied the opening of walking tracks in the 1890s and 1900s, has been sadly lacking in response to dedicated attempts by Jim Smith, Wilf Hilder and their enthusiastic helpers to rescue Lindeman Pass, Roberts Pass and Bruce's Walk from total oblivion.

For Frank Hurley, the Mountains could only be appreciated by walking them. By this, he did "not mean the amount of walking that is called for in getting from car or bus to this or that lookout. All true enjoyment must be paid for in effort. Only to those who have spent day after day clambering along ledges on the sheer cliff faces and descending tracks on the steep mountain-side into quiet glens where mosses and ferns cling to the dripping rocks and the majestic gums tower overhead, only to these people is the true spirit of the Mountains revealed."

Though many would concur with these sentiments, the revelation of "spirit" is an individual experience. It may come from quiet meditation on a sun-drenched rock, by tramping with a heavy pack for days at a time, in wonder at the playful spray of a waterfall on glistening rocks or the wheeling flight of an eagle, while scaling a vertical cliff face or gazing enraptured at a breathtaking panorama. The Blue Mountains offer a wealth of experiences like these, but challenges each of us to discover our own wilderness.

Margaret Baker

REFERENCES

Andrews, Alan E.J. *The Devil's Wilderness: George Caley's Journey to Mount Banks 1804* Blubberhead Press, 1984.

Baker, M.J., Corringham, R., Dark, J. *Native Plants of the Lower Blue Mountains* Three Sisters Productions, 1985.

Baker, M.J., Corringham, R., Dark, J. *Native Plants of the Upper Blue Mountains* Three Sisters Productions, 1984.

Barrallier, Francis "Journal of the Expedition into the Interior of New South Wales 1802".

Blackheath, Blue Mountains New South Wales, Described and Illustrated Blackheath Progress Committee, 1903.

The Blue Mountains: Katoomba and Leura Katoomba and Leura Tourist Association, 1903.

Blue Mountains Railway Tourist Guide Sydney, 1894.

"Blue Mountains Sights and Reserves" unpublished logbook, 1926.

Bowden, Miss Isobel "The Grose Valley Blackheath" in *Historic Blackheath* Rotary Club of Blackheath, 1976.

Burke, Anne "Awesome Cliffs, Fairy Dells and Lovers Silhouetted in the Sunset" in *The Blue Mountains: Grand Adventure for All* Stanbury and Bushell, Macleay Museum, University of Sydney, 1985.

Burke, Anne "Images of Popular Leisure in the Blue Mountains" unpublished thesis, Springwood Library, 1981.

Carter, H.J. *Gulliver in the Bush* Angus and Robertson, 1933.

Croft and Associates Pty. Ltd. and Walker, M. "Blue Mountains Heritage Study" Dept. of Environment and Planning/Blue Mountains City Council, 1985.

Darwin, Charles *The Voyage of the Beagle* Facsimile of 1831-1836 edition. Heron Books, Switzerland (no date).

Du Faur, Eccleston — Letter to Philadelphia Exhibition Commission, 1875.

Dunphy, Myles "The Blue Gum Forest Conservation Company 1931-32" in *Historic Blackheath* Rotary Club of Blackheath, 1976.

Else-Mitchell, R. "Bass's Land Explorations" *Journal of the Royal Australian Historical Society* XXXVII(IV), 1951:244-250

Flood, J. *Archaeology of the Dreamtime* Collins, 1983.

Govett, William Romain *Sketches of New South Wales Written and Illustrated for the Saturday Magazine 1836-1837* Gaston Renard, Melbourne, 1977.

Historic Blackheath Rotary Club of Blackheath, Katoomba, 1976.

Hurley, Frank *The Blue Mountains and Jenolan Caves* Angus & Robertson, 1952.

Lear, Margaret Rodriguez "He Came to Australia" unpublished thesis, Mitchell Library, 1967.

Low, John *The Giant Stairway 1932-1982* Blue Mountains City Library, 1982.

Mackaness, G. ed. *Fourteen Journeys over the Blue Mountains of New South Wales 1813-1841* Horwitz-Grahame, 1965.

Meredith, Mrs. C. (Louisa Ann) *Notes and Sketches of New South Wales During a Residence in that Colony from 1839 to 1844* Facsimile of 1844 edition. Ure Smith, 1973.

Myers, Francis *Coastal Scenery, Harbours, Mountains and Rivers of New South Wales* Govt. Printer, 1886.

Official Tourist Guidebook to Katoomba and Leura Katoomba Municipality (c.1910).

Ross, V.J. *The Everingham Letterbook: Letters of a First Fleet Convict* Anvil Press, 1985.

Smeaton, Oliphant *The Treasure Cave in the Blue Mountains* Oliphant, Anderson and Ferrier, Edinburgh and London (c.1900).

Spiers, Hugh *Landscape Art and the Blue Mountains* Alternative Publishing Co-op., 1981.

Stanbury, Peter and Bushell, Lydia eds. *The Blue Mountains: Grand Adventure for All* Macleay Museum, University of Sydney, 1985.

Streeton, Arthur — Letter to Frederick McCubbin, 1891.

Ward, Mel *Legend Walk : Australian Aboriginal Legends* Geoff Bates, 1979.

"I'm in the Blue Mountains boarding in a wee little cot for £1 a week. The sun is beautiful in the morning. He rises with me, he goes with me through the dewy forest, and is very intimate with me as I step through all the wondrous wild flowers. Birds chirp and whistle as I bare my white limbs to the first pure morning sunlight, and standing on a mossy sandstone rock gaze around and contemplate as my skin is gently warmed all over with the flood of sun. All around and above fine tall red gums, smooth of trunk as though cast in iron. The bloodwood, grey gum, turpentine tree, wattle, and all sorts of flowers in their best summer array. Below me runs a crystal virgin brook with a rocky bottom and rushes flourishing, tickling me and having great fun as I step gently into the cold, clear water, one foot, then the other; I splash the water high over my head; it descends in hundreds of gems; dry myself with nice towel on the sunny rock; shake my hair about in the sun to dry, and into my bright striped pyjamas and back to breakfast."

Arthur Streeton, 1891

Jamison Valley, towards Broken Rock Range

"Beyond is more of vastness; a huge dark veiled in the blue mist which deepens with every mile of distance."

Francis Myers, 1886

Megalong and Kanimbla Valleys under snow clouds

"And as the sky is covered you may see the yellow and brown cliff faces change to dull cold grey. The forest in the depths becomes black and all the blue mists ghastly as the avant couriers of the storm."

    Francis Myers, 1886

Grose Valley

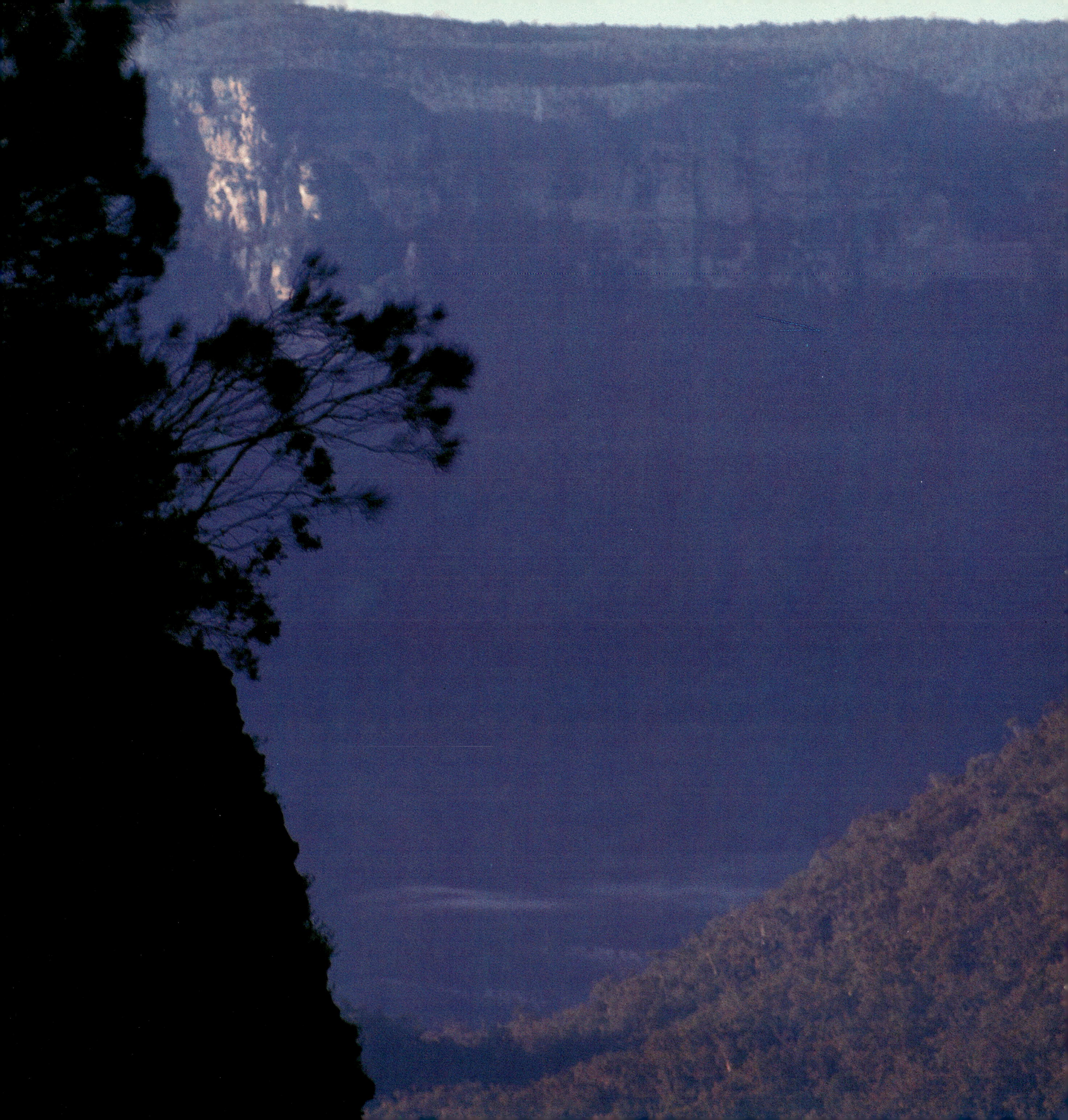

West from Narrow Neck

"No one had ever reached these hills. Beyond them lay China the poor Irish convicts had once thought."

                Alan Andrews, 1984

West from Narrow Neck

"...and through all the summer months frequent thunder, as if the spirits who had wrought their mounds below were still toiling at some other labour in mid air"

    Francis Myers, 1886

Head of the old landslide, Katoomba

Grose Valley

"The effect of the clarity and purity of the atmosphere is to be noticed upon visitors from the lowlands at once. It induces sleep for the first few hours. Then it produces a wonderful energy that keeps visitors, who are usually of sedentary habits, moving about with surprising ease and activity. It also makes the worst-toned dinner bell into a sweet musical instrument by its alchemy."

Official Tourist Guidebook to Katoomba and Leura, c.1910

Jamison Valley, towards Narrow Neck

"Cliff faces leagues long, and a thousand feet perpendicular; huge basins, like veritable gulfs in space where a firmament of blue gathers between the rocky mountain head and the first growth below."

Francis Myers, 1886

Sandstone cliffs, Wall's Ledge

The Three Sisters

Jamison Valley and National Pass

"...an immense gulf unexpectedly opens through the trees which border the pathway, at a depth of perhaps 1500 feet. Walking on a few yards, one stands on the brink of a vast precipice, and below one sees a grand bay or gulf, for I know not what other name to give it, thickly covered with forest."

                Charles Darwin, 1836

Headland, Narrow Neck

"The holiday crowd rarely travel more than half a mile along the lovely [Narrow Neck] promontory. Beyond this there are miles of good walking and views which few men have been privileged to gaze upon. About two and a half miles out on this great ridge (which forms a natural barrier of colossal proportions between the Jamison and Megalong Valleys) the writer and two others discovered one of the most splendid amphitheatres ever seen. Observations of its beauty had to be taken from the trunk of a fallen tree which hung twenty feet over the chasm fully a thousand feet deep."

Official Tourist Guidebook, c.1910

West from Narrow Neck

Rice flowers (Pimelea linifolia) *eastern Grose Valley*

Western Grose Valley

"In 1859 the whole length of the Grose was surveyed by a party of sappers to ascertain if it could be used as a line for the railway, but the decision was that the terrain was too unsuitable."

    Miss Isobel Bowden, 1976

Grose Valley, looking east

"Timber! There is enough timber here to build the cities of the world!"

Official Tourist Guidebook, c.1910

Mt. Banks

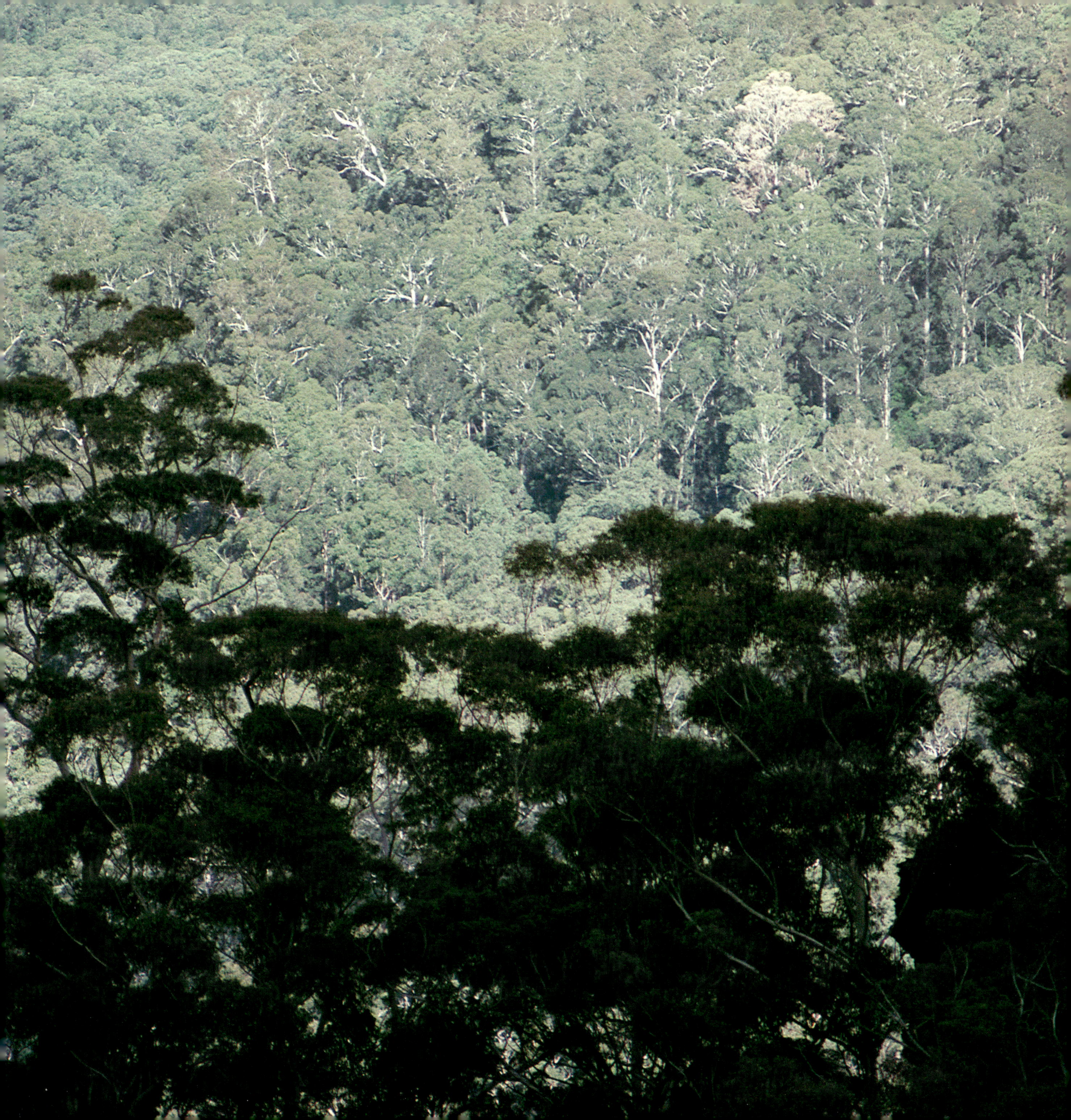

Sublime Point, Jamison Valley

"The work of making the track to the bottom of Govetts Leap...was deemed to be an impossibility by all the residents and expert mountaineers, as the track would have to be cut into the perpendicular cliffs. Nothing daunted however by these pessimists, ...Mr. Williams proceded to work. Through his perserverance and skill with explosives he succeeded at last after seven months of hard and dispirited work as could be thought of."

    Margaret Rodriguez Lear, 1967

Stairway, Govett's Leap

Diamond Falls, Narrow Neck

Lookout, Prince Henry Cliff Walk

"Taken from above the lookout, the view is actually of the lookout itself; the image of a view of a view of a lookout."

Anne Burke, 1981, referring to postcards by Kitch & Co.

Jamison Valley headland

"I propose, with a few members of the New South Wales Academy of Arts, to endeavour, during the spring to collate a portfolio of Blue Mountains scenery …(to be taken by pencil and camera). I propose leaving Sydney on Thursday next, for a week."

            Eccleston Du Faur, 1875

Split rock, Du Faur's Head

Diamond Falls, Narrow Neck

Diamond Falls, Narrow Neck

"Blessed be God for the mountains"
                Francis Myers, 1886

"o'er mountain routes
and over wild wolds clouded up with
brush,
and cut with marshes perilously deep, —
so they went forth at dawn;"

Charles Harpur "The Creek
of the Four Graves", 1868

Hanging swamp, Blackheath

Narrow Neck headland

Wind-eroded Cave

"On a short walk to the west is a large cave formed by overhanging rocks, where the sand formations of the sedimentary sandstone have been etched into relief by wind over thousands of years."

Blackheath, 1903

Diamond Falls at sunset

"...and out on the unforested heaths, rich lights of purple and gold shall be enkindled."

Francis Myers, 1886

Rock face from Little Zig-Zag

Rock form, Narrow Neck

"But all beyond the great Fault stood firm, and lifting a bold face to all the influences of all the years which ploughed out the thunderous gorges, isolated the peaks and obelisks and bared the cliffs. Nature wrought greatly here."

                Francis Myers, 1886

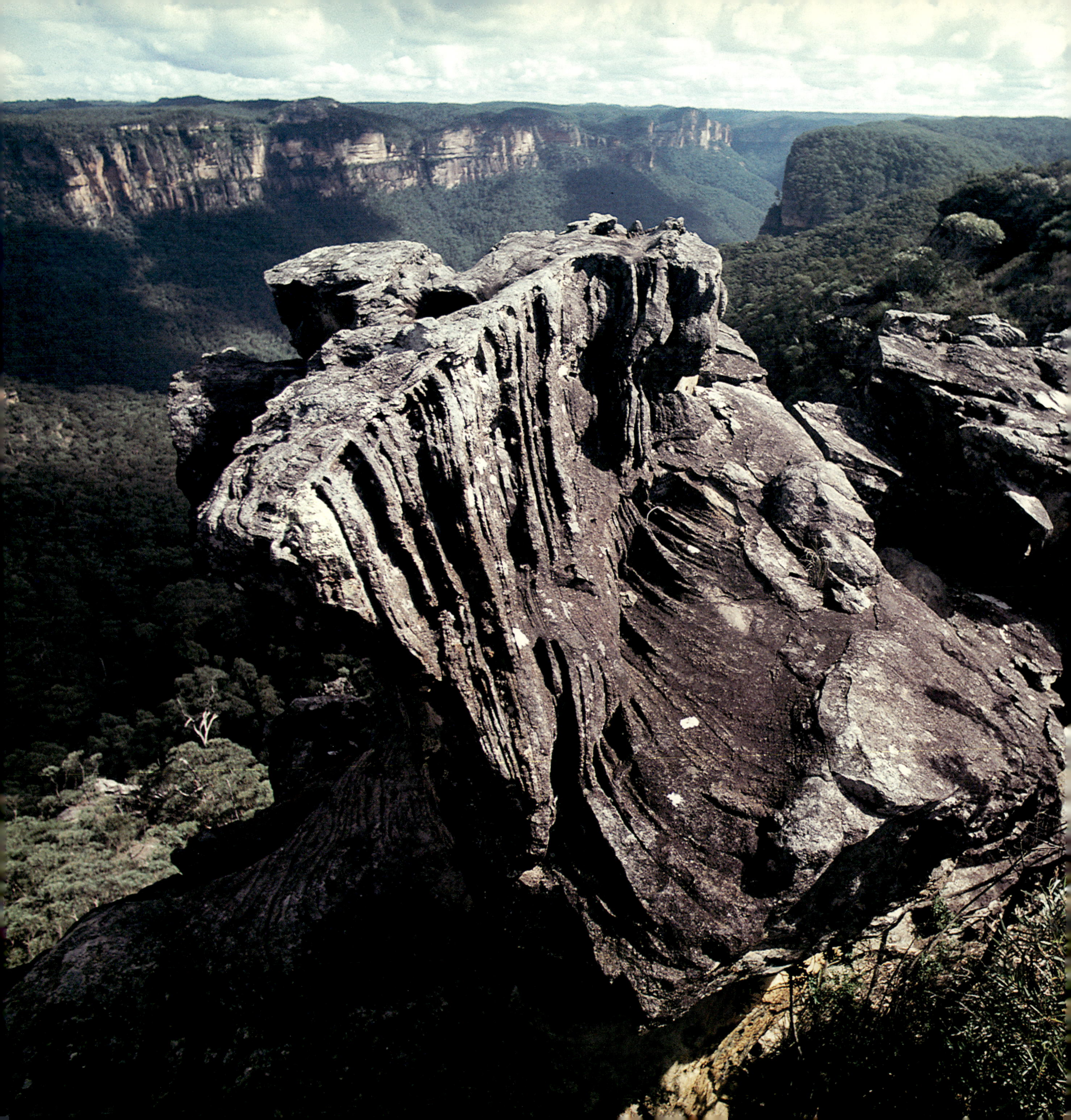

Sublime Point

From Mt. Banks

Rock form, Narrow Neck

From Mt. Banks

"We gazed at it awhile with aweful reverence of that God by whom all things are made, we then left the precipice and continued our route along the green ridge abovementioned."

            Mathew Everingham, 1795

Rock form, Mt. Banks

Berghofer's Pass sign pecked away during WW1

Narrow Neck silhouette

Northern Grose Valley

"The hunt of the previous day had procured good meals for my men, and was instrumental in making them regain their good spirits.
In the evening I went for a bathe in the river."

    Francis Barrallier, at Kanangra, 1802

Valley near Katoomba

Smooth Barked Apple (Angophora costata) *Wall's Ledge*

Mountain Ash (Eucalyptus Oreades) *Little Zig-Zag*

Mountain Blue Gum (Eucalyptus deanei) *Blue Gum Forest*

Blue Gum Forest

Smooth Barked Apple (Angophora costata)

Smooth Barked Apple (Angophora costata)

"Steam arose from the warm ground and the tall shafts and their extended company well up aloft bore a well-washed appearance as about an inch of rain had drummed down."

    Myles Dunphy, "The Blue Gum Forest Conservation Company 1931-32"

Trees, Narrow Neck

Black Ash (Eucalyptus sieberi)

Track, Katoomba

Rock-eating tree, Kings Tableland

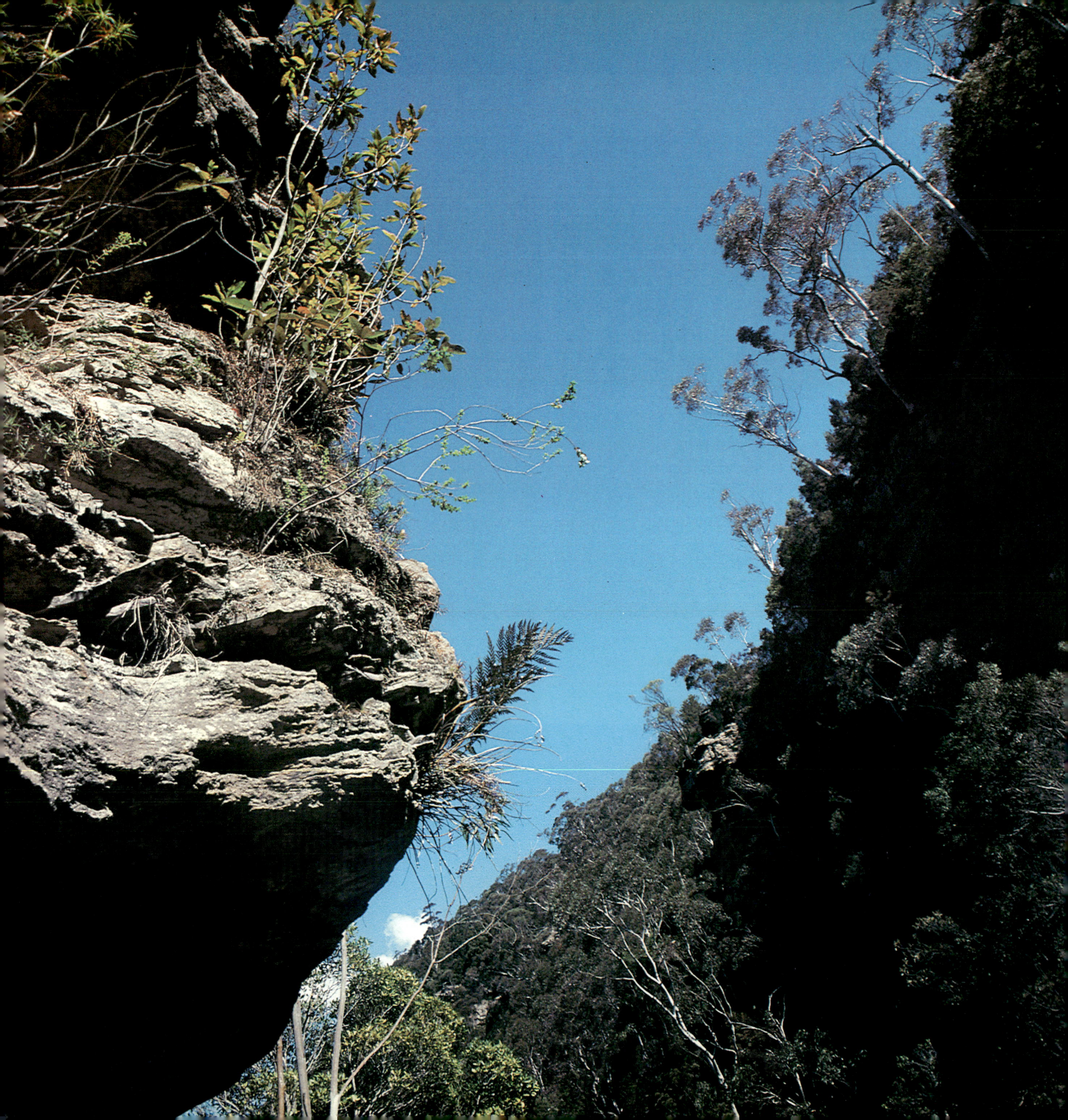

"Looking upward is to behold a sight most awe inspiring, superb specimens of natural architectural beauty in huge rocks rearing aloft their frowning eminences and forming coverings through which the sun's rays never penetrate."

The Blue Mountains: Katoomba and Leura, 1903

Trees and ferns, Blackheath

Shipley Plateau, Blackheath

Hillside regenerating after fire

Federal Pass, Jamison Valley

"The Committee (for the Conservation of the Blue Gum Forest) found the going very hard; the time being towards the end of the Depression was bad for this sort of thing. Several Blue Gum Balls and Austen Socials helped out. Miss Dorothy Lawry and the Committee compiled a booklet on walking tours."

                    Miss Isobel Bowden, 1976

Blue Gum Forest and Grose Valley

Rock Pool, Wall's Ledge

Den Fenella, circular staircase carved in stone

"When the place was smaller and before the advent of local government...when the town people all joined heartily in the work, of developing the town, ...most of the sights were opened by local subscription, e.g. Rodriguez Pass, and voluntary labour — Grand Canyon, Centennial Glen, Porter's Pass and Hargraves lookout, Mermaid's Cave (Govett's Walk) the track to the Horseshoe Falls".

Blue Mountains Sights and Reserves, 1926

Stone steps, Centennial Glen

Path across Greaves Creek

"Past this fern-clad slope you may wander on, meandering with the water of the brook; the great hills on either side towering aloft from the rich dark, moss-grown feet of the creek to bare-headed summits, where the crags glow and the lizard crouches, silent, motionless, ugly and harmless."

Francis Myers, 1886

Neates Glen

Gladstone Pass

King Ferns (Todea barbara) Gladstone Pass

The Jungle, Grose Valley

"A vale of beauty lovelier than all the valleys of the great hills"

Francis Myers, 1886

Water Ferns and Filmy Ferns, Gladstone Pass

Fan Fern (Sticherus sp.)

Ferns and mosses, Asmodeus Pool

Neates Glen, Blackheath

"Within the shadows of the natural rock chamber, every species of fern flourishes in rich profusion"

    Official Tourist Guidebook, c.1910

Petrophile sp., *algae and lichens, Kings Tableland*

Young Tree Ferns

Coral Fern (Gleichenia dicarpa) *in frost*

Water Ferns, Kanimbla Valley

"...crag fronts rise sheer from rent chasms of dreadful gloom, and where gentler banks sheltered from every blast, raise beauties of frond and leaf in palm and fern, such as are never equalled and never excelled"

    Francis Myers, 1886

"The golden yellows of delicate fronds relieve with wonderful grace the red greys of the rock, draping the geological hardness with shimmering silken softness."

Official Tourist Guidebook, c.1910

Water Ferns on basalt rock ledge

"A rare Australian conifer surviving from Gondwanaland ... a tenuous existence in the spray of a few Blue Mountains waterfalls."

Jim Smith, ecologist, 1985

Microstrobos fitzgeraldii *under Wentworth Falls*

Katoomba Falls in ice

"Katoomba is admitted to be one of the healthiest spots in the world, and is constantly recommended by the faculty to people suffering from any lung complaint."

Tourist Guide to the Blue Mountains, 1887

Ant nest in snow, Blackheath

Cave, Wollangambe River

Convoluted rock, Lockley's Pylon

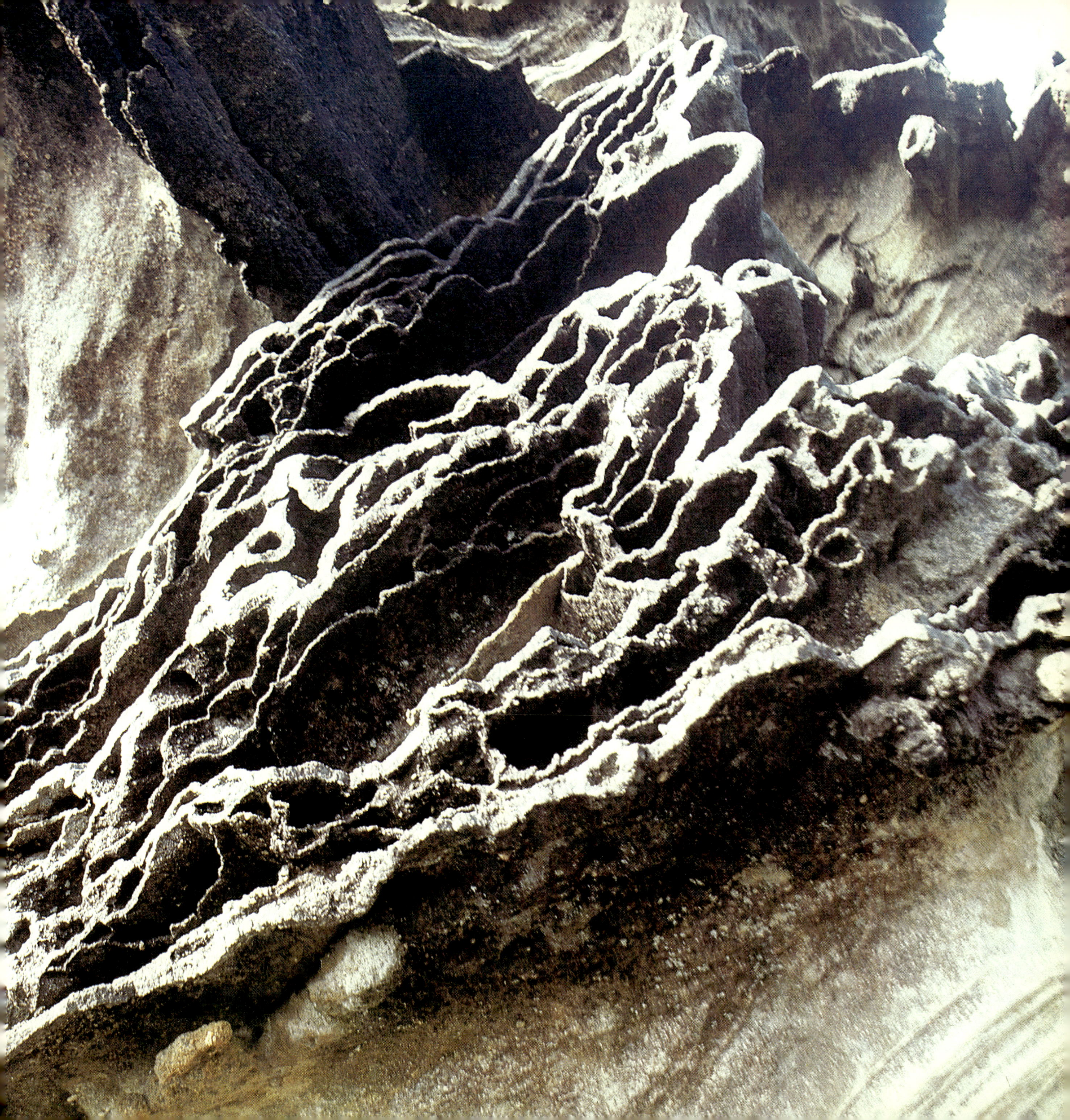

Natural rock, Shipley Plateau

Earth-spirit rock form, McMahon's Point Lookout

Stone embankment, Berghofer's Pass

Reinit's Pass

Lichens, moss and leaves

"...on the lap of lands unseen
within a secret zone
There shine diviner gold and green
than man has ever known."

          Henry Kendall "Orara", 1879

Rainforest rock

Lichens and rock, Jamison Valley

Lichens and rock, Grose Valley

Rock form, Kings Tableland

Lichens and rock, Porter's Pass

Sandstone overhang, Mt. Victoria

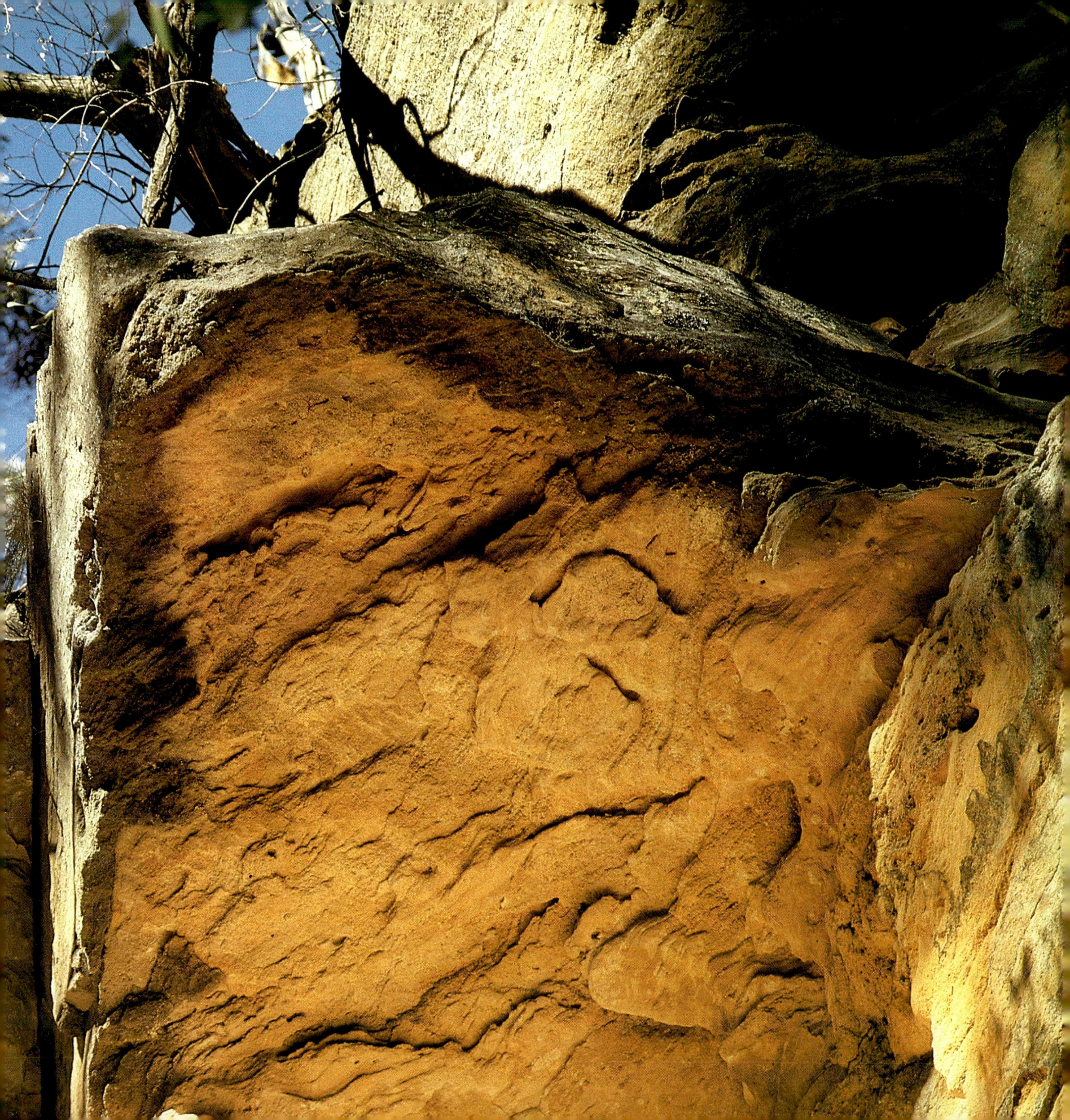

Decaying log, Reinit's Pass

Wet bark, Warragamba

Ironstone shakes after fire

Lichens, moss and leaves

Ice and leaves, Katoomba

Weathered log, Wollangambe River

Smooth Barked Apple (Angophora costata)

Monkey Gum (Eucalyptus cypellocarpa)

Smooth Barked Apple (Angophora costata)

Mountain Blue Gum (Eucalyptus deanei)

Scribbly Gum (Eucalyptus sclerophylla)

Mountain Blue Gum (Eucalyptus deanei)

New eucalypt shoots

Picturesque inhabitant of waterfall spray zone

Sydney Peppermint (Eucalyptus piperita) *coppicing after fire*

Wet cliff face with ferns and lilies

Forest floor after rain

"When the storm is over and put, go forth and taste of the sweetness the beautiful rain has brought. And in the bush all the dear balsamic odours shall be set free."

        Francis Myers, 1886

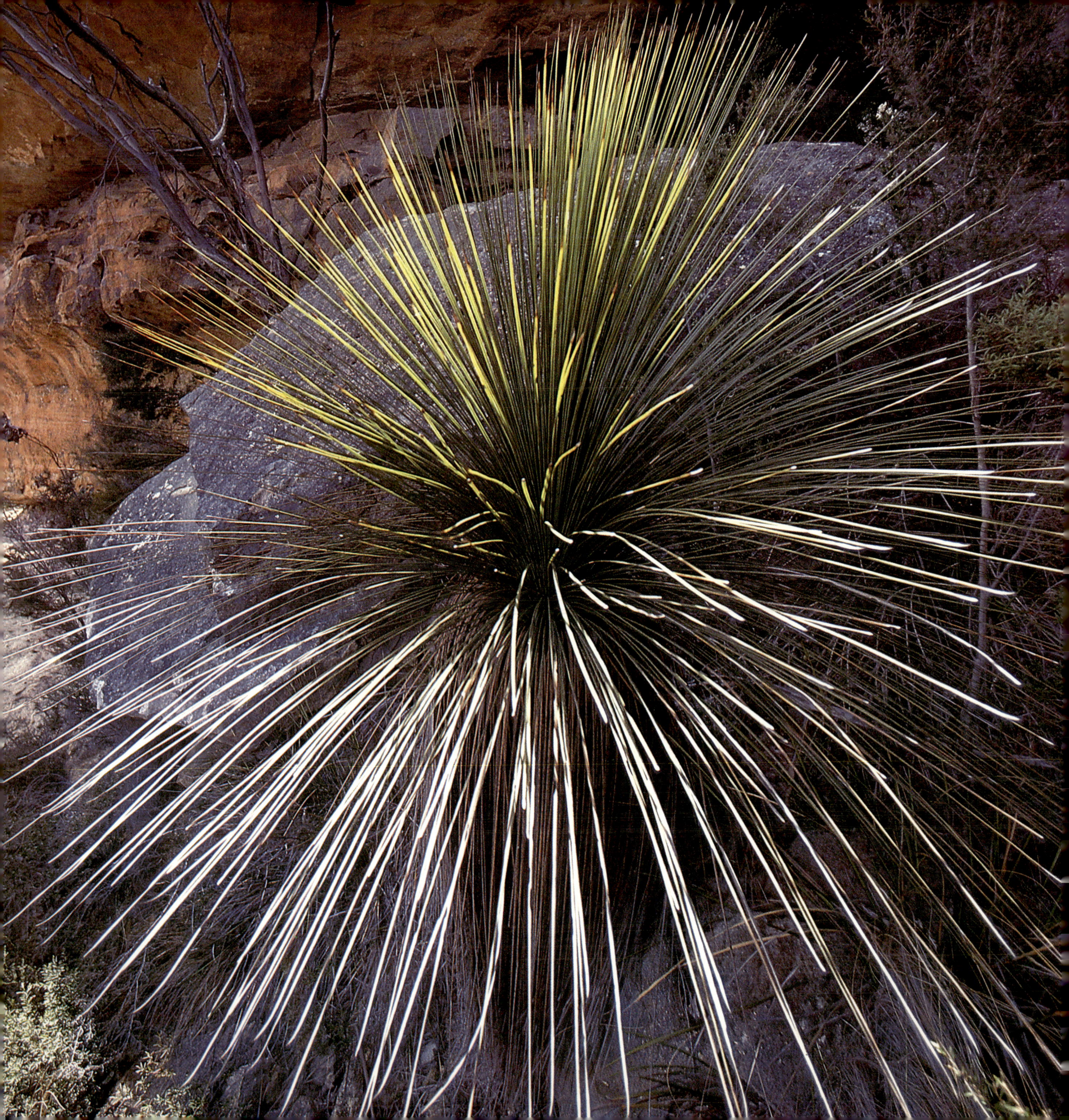

Broad-leaved Geebung (Persoonia levis)

Forest fungi under Govett's Leap

Insect-eating Forked Sundew (Drosera binata)

Grass Tree, Porter's Pass

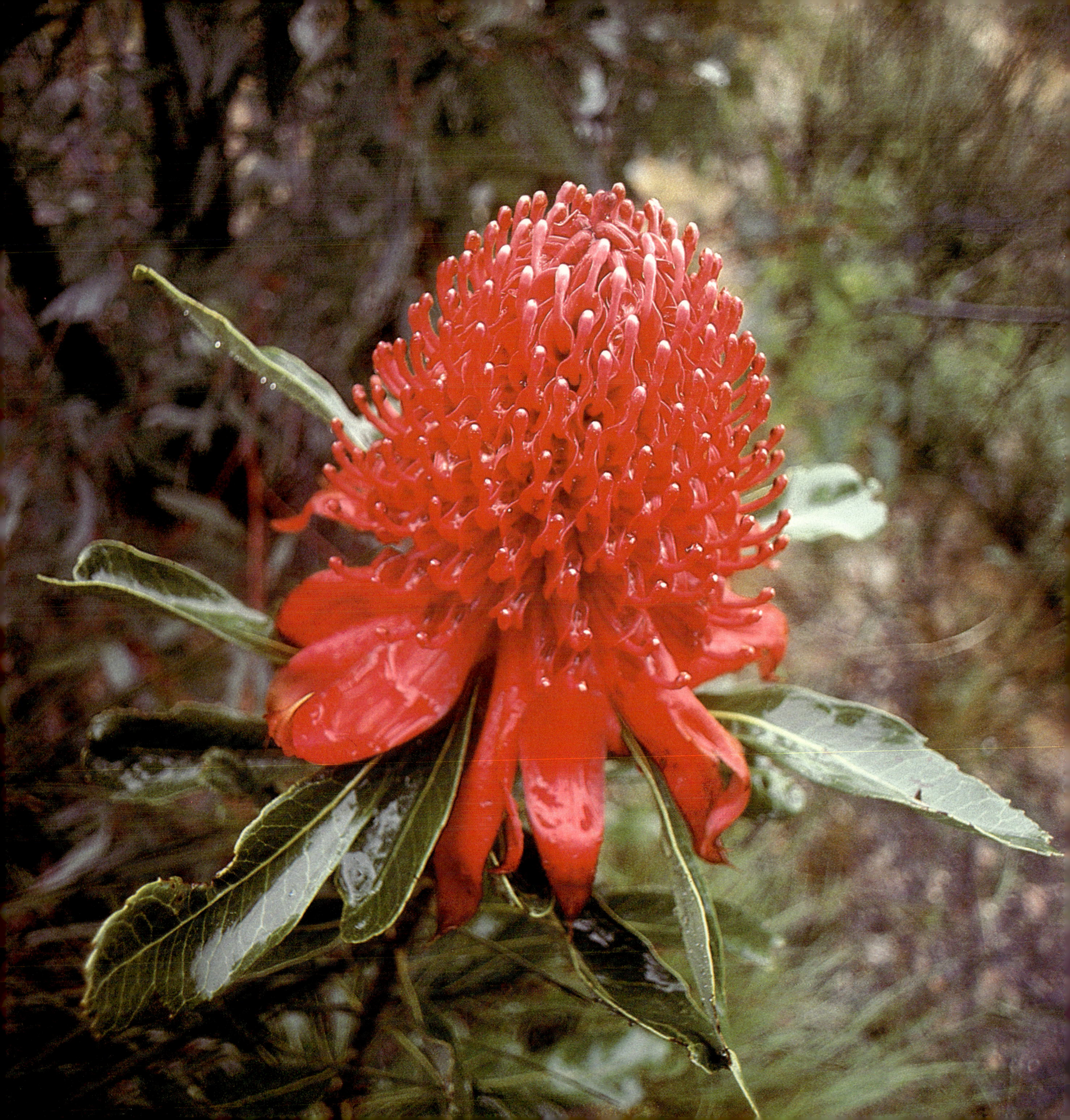

Boronia ledifolia

Drumsticks (Isopogon anemonifolius)

Kunzea capitata

Sunshine wattle (Acacia terminalis)

"Also in that divine atmosphere, the more regular moisture from light showers and early morning mist with less evaporation, makes the flowering finer and apparently more attractive."

                H.J. Carter, 1933

"The tall waratahs beam even brighter amongst the fragrant undergrowth."

                Francis Myers, 1886

Waratah (Telopea speciossisima)

Sunshine wattle (Acacia terminalis)

Insect-eating Sundew (Drosera spathulata)

Sprengelia monticola

"Spring! How can anyone venture to try to put spring into words when one flower or song of bird is so immeasurably more eloquent of the spirit and the beauty of it. The spring-birth warms the blood...it whets the appetite to be out, if only for an hour, in the fairyland of the wild."

Archer Russell, 1944

Old timber in Berghofer's Pass embankment

Young Waratahs (Telopea speciossisima)

Drumsticks (Isopogon anemonifolius)

Boronia ledifolia

Sprengelia incarnata

Schelhammera undulata

Epacris obtusifolia

Mountain Devil (Lambertia formosa)

Wattle (Acacia sp.)

Native holly (Oxylobium ilicifolium)

Rice flower (Pimelea linifolia)

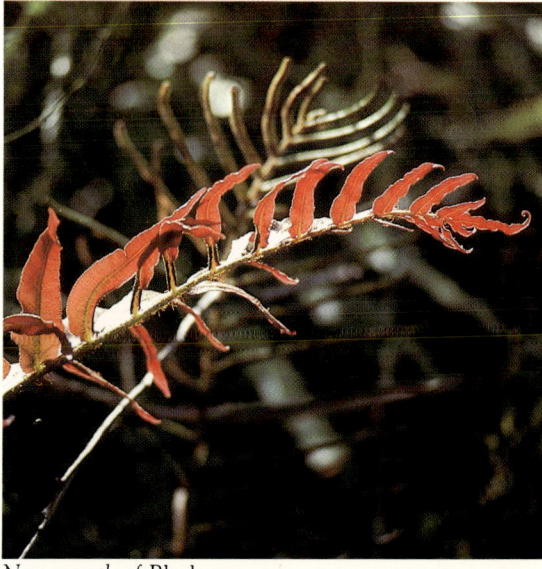

New growth of Blechnum sp.

Epacris microphylla

Grevillea acanthifolia

Dianella sp.

Patersonia longifolia

Guinea flower (Hibbertia sp.)

Zieria laevigata

Drumsticks (Isopogon anemonifolius)

Woollsia pungens

Hibbertia dentata

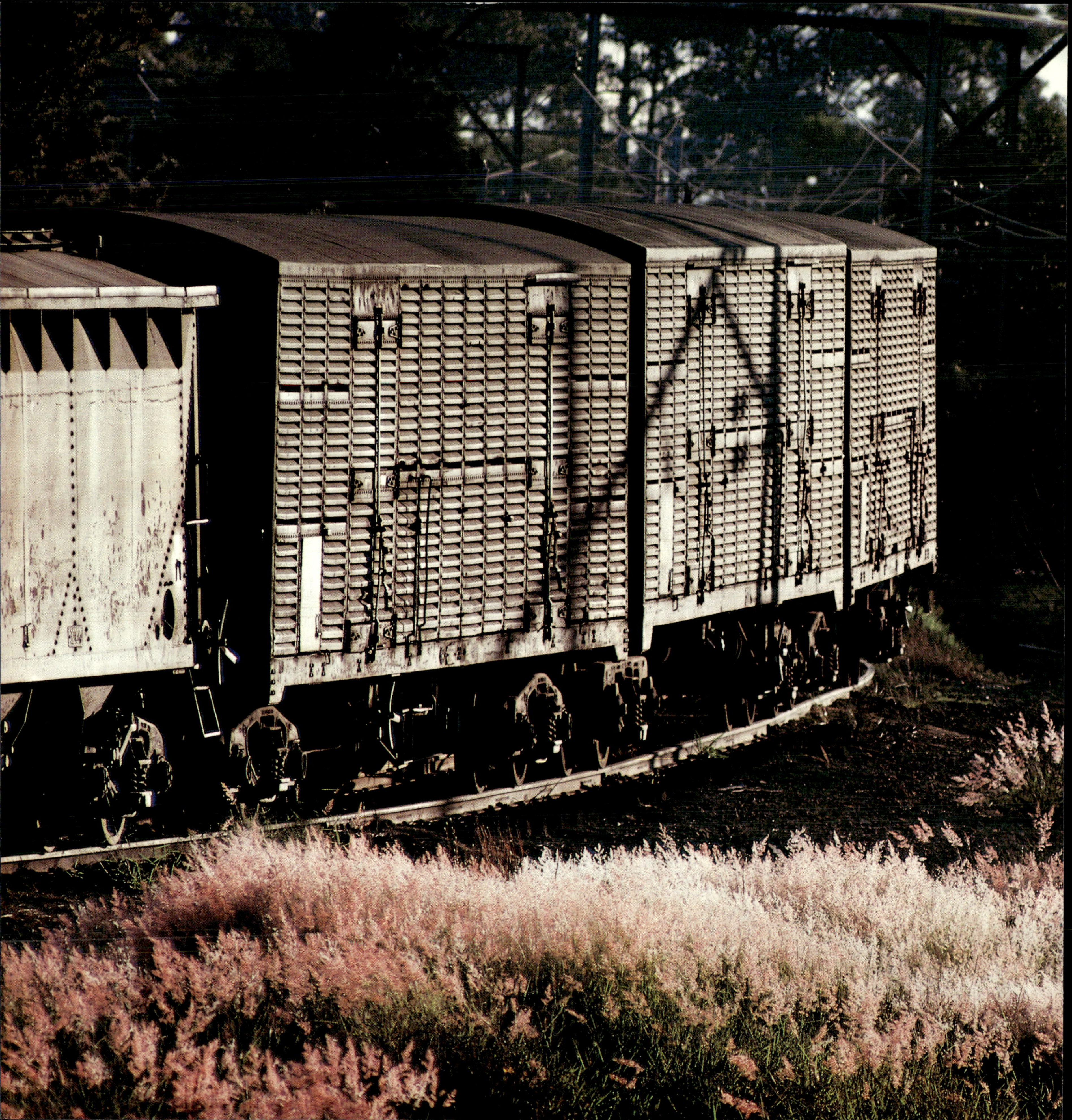

"As there are few passenger trains, travellers between small Mountain stations must accustom themselves to a luggage train. Those who are content to use this means can travel at the tail end of a luggage train at almost any hour of the day."

The Blue Mountains, 1903

"The new venture, which is known as the Chert Road Metal and Timber Pty. Ltd., with an Authorised Capital of £30,000, is constructing a tramway 25 chains in length, capable of carrying 60 tons of broken metal per hour. The company has received permission to construct a railway siding adjacent to the quarry with every facility for direct handling."

Blue Mountains Echo 6th April 1923

Rail trucks and Nepal grass, Valley Heights

Funicular railway cutting, Mt. Victoria

Wentworth Falls from National Pass

"The most remarkable of the cascades is ...that which falls into the head of the Grose River, which the Surveyor General named Govett's Leap from the circumstances of my first having come upon the spot."

    William Romain Govett, c.1835

Govett's Leap

"The scenery is full of grandeur, and to add to its beauty there are two streams, which are precipitated into the mighty chasm, and although meeting no impediment but the atmosphere in their descent, they are dissipated into mist long before their waters can reach the bottom"

The Railway Guide to New South Wales, 1884

Base of Govett's Leap

"A track from the Valley of the Waters to Wentworth Falls was begun in 1890. Captain Murray, the engineer, devised the means of building into the cliff-face by letting a man over the cliff on a rope to mark the plan of the stairs on the rock."

Anne Burke, 1981

Jamison Creek at Wentworth Falls

Jamison Creek at Weeping Rock

"Is there, ah is there a land...
Seen through a cloud's sudden rift,
Where all the rainbows of Time
Slowly and silently drift?"

    Ethel Turner "The Rainbow", 1905

Wentworth Falls

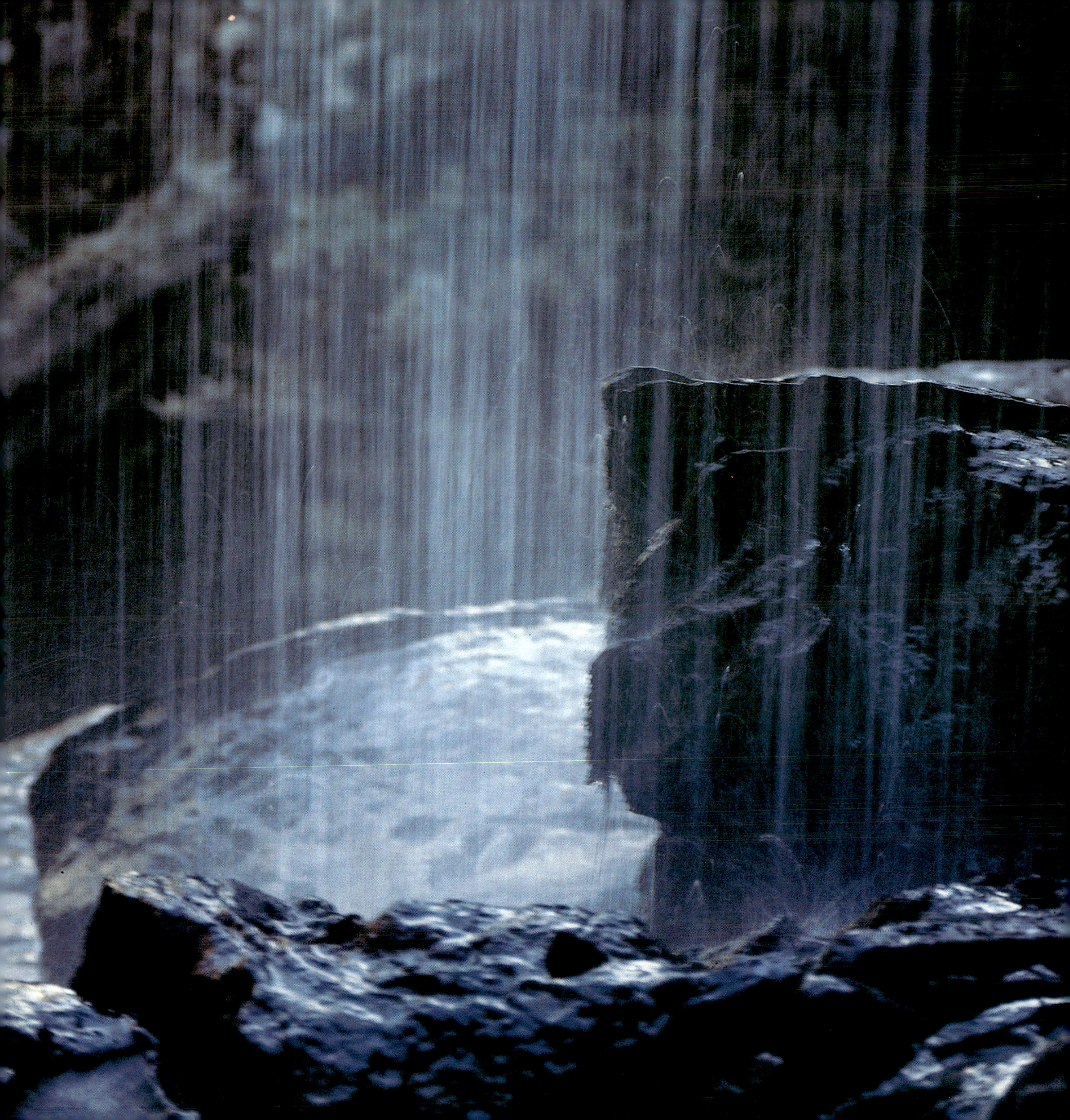

Valley of the Waters Creek, Asmodeus Pool

Valley of the Waters

Jamison Creek

Sylvia Falls, Valley of the Waters

"...hemmed in by frowning brown cliffs, from ledges which drip gentle streams whilst ferns revelling on the moisture grow on the face of the rocks."

The Blue Mountains, 1903

Wentworth Falls

Porter's Pass

113

Sylvia Falls

Waterfall, Federal Pass

Gladstone Pass

"All around the gentle gurgle of the waters and dainty rustling of the trees and ferns lends a pretty charm to the scene."

The Blue Mountains, 1903

Creek, Shipley Plateau

Wet steps, Valley of the Waters

Rodriguez Pass

"Deep calling unto deep in innumerable waterfalls."

Francis Myers, 1886

Wollangambe River

Sunrise, Grose River

Wentworth Falls

Cox's River

Valley of the Waters Creek

"To me these mountains have never ceased to supply perennial cause of intense interest; and some forty years of exploration have not exhausted the variety and the number of such interests."

    H.J. Carter, 1933

Diamond Creek

Valley of the Waters

119

water-worn rock, Greaves Creek

Neates Glen

Wentworth Falls

Wentworth Falls

Grose Valley

Den Fenella

"The stream that, crooning to itself,
Comes down a tireless rover,
Flows calmly to the rocky shelf,
And there leaps bravely over."

Henry Lawson "The Blue Mountains",
                              1888

Katoomba Creek

Govett's Leap Brook

"The Blue Gum Forest (Reserve 63, 521 for public recreation) was notified on 2nd September 1932, and the Regulations were published in Government Gazette of 2nd March 1934"

    Miss Isobel Bowden, 1976

Grose River and Blue Gum bridge

"The stream no longer foams and bubbles in headlong course, but glides in long glistening reaches."

The Blue Mountains, 1903

River still life

"The main valley... had a fine rill of water, which I could hear tumbling down the rocks a little higher up."

George Caley, 1804

Steam from the rising sun

"You are perhaps aware...that in some remote part of the Blue Mountains an enormously rich treasure had been hidden by a number of convicts, who were afterwards caught, but refused to declare the secret, which died with them."

                Oliphant Smeaton, c.1900

Sand bar reflections

"The water's over Nattai Bridge —
The last mail has been run."

Old Jack Martin of Camden, on the
rising waters of Lake Burragorang, 1964

Lake Burragorang